Haunted Albuquerque

HAUNTED ALBUQUERQUE

CODY POLSTON

Published by Haunted America
A division of The History Press
Charleston, SC
www.historypress.com

Copyright © 2021 by Cody Polston
All rights reserved

First published 2021

Manufactured in the United States

ISBN 9781467149785

Library of Congress Control Number: 2021938372

Notice: The information in this book is true and complete to the best of our knowledge. It is offered without guarantee on the part of the author or The History Press. The author and The History Press disclaim all liability in connection with the use of this book.

All rights reserved. No part of this book may be reproduced or transmitted in any form whatsoever without prior written permission from the publisher except in the case of brief quotations embodied in critical articles and reviews.

CONTENTS

Preface	7
1. A City Divided	9
2. The KiMo Theater	18
3. The Wool Warehouse Theater	32
4. The Hotel Andaluz	43
5. The Albuquerque Press Club	55
6. The Old Bernalillo County Courthouse	61
7. Mount Calvary Cemetery	66
8. Old Albuquerque High School	75
9. Fairview Cemetery	82
10. Haunted Hill	92
11. The Albuquerque Little Theatre	98
12. Ghostlore	107
Bibliography	119
About the Author	123

Preface

Many years ago, I wrote a book called *The Ghosts of Old Town Albuquerque* to share the myriad interesting ghost stories that abound in the heart of the Duke City. However, there are many other supernatural tales spanning across the city, thus the need for this book to cover the remaining legends and folklore that lie in the other sections of Albuquerque.

Since I was a young child, I have loved tales about the supernatural and the paranormal, which eventually led to a fascination with horror films.

Why do I love ghost stories? Because like horror movies, they provide a temporary sort of terror, yet you know that you are safe. People go to horror films because they want to be frightened or they wouldn't do it twice. You choose your entertainment because you want it to affect you. I can watch a horror film like *Nightmare on Elm Street* and enjoy the movie, even though I know that the film's villain, Freddy Krueger, isn't real. The same is true with ghost stories. I really appreciate them, especially if there is some historical element attached to the story. However, like horror movies, if the conversation changes to a discussion about if the stories are true, that is another matter. In that regard, ghost stories must be taken with a grain of salt.

One of the characteristics that distinguish ghost stories from other forms of folklore is that they emphasize the mystery and the inconclusive, which invites various kinds of interpretation. From my perspective, the answer to the question "Do you believe?" belongs to the people who are telling or listening to a story of a paranormal experience. They decide to want to

Preface

believe or even if they're going to engage with it concerning any type of belief at all. What I do is take the paranormal narratives seriously. I pay attention to them and treat them analytically. It is that love of ghost stories that gives me additional insight. I become fascinated by the elements of the stories themselves. How were they created? Why do some last while others are forgotten? How do they morph over time as they pass from one storyteller to another? The combination of these interests drew me into the hobby of ghost hunting and, eventually, my own ghost hunting team, the Southwest Ghost Hunter's Association (SGHA).

It is essential to understand that there is a difference between "ghost stories" and "personal paranormal encounters." Ghost stories are just that—stories. They revolve around a central character that usually undergoes some traumatic event, explaining why they are haunting a particular location. Ghost stories are told with a dramatic fervor with spooky anecdotes and ambiance. They primarily serve as entertainment and are dependent on the ability of the storyteller to be effective.

However, personal paranormal encounters are quite different. Typically, they are told reluctantly and with an apology. The teller is often aware that such admissions are considered to be the delusions of a troubled mind and is mindful of being judged. Of course, there is no actual witness stand. Yet people who have these encounters are conscious of the possibility of being judged irrational and assume a stance that anticipates the skepticism of their observations and conclusions.

In these instances, I do not doubt that the person had an experience. Obviously, they did, but it is their interpretation of the circumstances and the environment that I tend to ponder and open up for discussion.

Many of the supernatural tales in this book are a combination of both types. They are ghost stories that are mixed with personal paranormal encounters. As such, I have included additional insights for those who are more inquisitive. I hope that you enjoy reading about these fascinating places as much as I did researching and writing about them.

1
A CITY DIVIDED

The mighty Rio Grande River has played a significant role in Albuquerque's history. In its early days, the floods that came each spring menaced portions of the city. Melting snow in the Colorado mountains and spring rains often caused the river to reach flood stage, which flooded all of the low-lying areas in the river bottoms near the town. In the early days of the city, the Rio Grande often established a new course, breaking through its banks upstream. Sometimes this caused the river to pass through the center of the original townsite. Because of the threat of flooding, the railroad could not be constructed near Old Town. So, the railroad developers moved the tracks several miles to the east, where the enterprise would be safe from those natural hazards.

On April 22, 1880, an official celebration began with a parade led by the Ninth Cavalry Band from Santa Fe. A proud Franz Huning followed in his carriage, along with the carriages of other speakers and prominent citizens. Then came schoolchildren, horseback riders with decorated bridles and saddles and, finally, citizens in their Sunday best, either walking or riding their burros. They followed a road that Huning himself had improved from the plaza to the railroad tracks that would be called Railroad Avenue and, later, Central. Arriving at the tracks, the crowd surrounded two flatcars pulled in as an impromptu stage, where speakers delivered flowery oratory in both Spanish and English. Huning was the first to speak, praising the railroad and sharing his high expectations for Albuquerque's future development. Other speakers included Miguel Otero, by then a vice president of AT&SF, and

Hazeldine, who asked, "Are we of Albuquerque prepared to take advantage of this opportunity?" And the band played on.

Then the crowd climbed aboard a ten-car excursion train covered in red, white and blue banners for a free trip to Bernalillo. The thirty-minute ride, traveling faster than most of its riders ever had before, was the experience of a lifetime for many, especially the poor people of Albuquerque. In Bernalillo, visitors were treated to another celebration with more speeches led, ironically, by José Leandro Perea and a fiesta with tables covered with food and drink. Back in Albuquerque, revelers hurried back to the plaza for more festivities. Barrels of wine awaited them at the plaza. The military band played, artillery boomed and fireworks sparkled in the night sky. Father Donato Gasparri gave the final speech, pointing out that Albuquerque was the "heart and center" of the New Mexico Territory.

The sleepy little village of Albuquerque wasn't then the heart and center of the territory, but because of the railroad, it soon would be. The railroad created a second town, as saloons and stores were erected next to the railroad tracks in tents and shacks. In time, the newly formed commercial district gained permanent structures of brick and stone. It became known as New Town, and the original community became Old Town. The day after the grand celebration, Peter "Shorty" Parker established the first business in New Town, where the dirt road now named Railroad Avenue crossed the tracks. He paced off six square feet, which he claimed by squatter's rights. Next, he dug a hole in the sand to keep his merchandise cool. With several broken boards and a barrel, he had a counter and opened his bar for business. The Concannon House soon opened for business in two spacious tents next to the tracks and south of Shorty's establishment. Lots were selling for ten dollars each. Land speculators, opportunists, businessmen and professionals began arriving. A cluster of tents, shanties and even a few frame and adobe buildings began to rise along Railroad Avenue. To link Old Town and New Town, the Street Railway Co. was organized in 1880.

The railroad also brought "undesirables," including gamblers and the first prostitutes. By the late 1800s, the city had twenty saloons, multiple gambling houses and brothels, which called themselves "wine rooms." The red-light district was established along Third and Fourth Streets between Copper and Tijeras. Train robberies and gunfights were not uncommon, and most citizens carried pistols. Vigilantes hanged many an outlaw and horse thief during these wild years.

In the 1880s, Albuquerque also had opium dens. There were campaigns not to close them but to move them off Central Avenue, which was called

Looking down First Street in 1908. *Library of Congress.*

Looking east down Central Street in 1943. *Library of Congress.*

Railroad Avenue back then, to Gold or Silver. Fortunately, the railroad also attracted reliable businesspeople. They intended to have safe, respectable homes for their wives and children and an environment that would appeal to homebuilders. After many years, Albuquerque had become a comparatively peaceful place. Even after the railroad's coming, there was even more lawlessness for a while, but things quieted down within a few years, and the outlaws moved on to wilder places. In 1889, Albuquerque won a rather heated battle for the right to locate the state university in the city.

The trolley was the pride of Albuquerque. It was powered by eight mule-drawn cars along three miles of track that connected the Old Town plaza with New Town and the suburb of Barelas. Its president was Oliver E. Cromwell, whose financial backers were Huning and Hazeldine. Passengers could ride in the open cars from the railroad depot to the end of the line at Elias Stover's house near the plaza. The light, narrow-gauge tracks ran down the center of Railroad Avenue on an elevated grade of dirt. Cars were so light that high winds often blew them off the tracks, which required riders and the conductor to lift them back on again. There was a rush hour each morning and evening when workers commuted to and from the railroad yards, but the trolley operated at a slower pace the rest of the time. Drivers often waited for shoppers to finish their errands. Anyone who lacked a fare could charge it. The founders of New Town hoped that New Town and Old Town would grow together and become one, but almost two miles of bare floodplain separated them. The tall buildings of New Town and the low adobe buildings of Old Town just didn't fit together and neither did attitudes and cultures. The two towns clashed for years over the right to postmark their mail Albuquerque. From Washington, the post office decreed that they would use Old Albuquerque and New Albuquerque. Old Town wasn't formally incorporated into Albuquerque until 1949.

The Town Company hired Colonel Walter G. Marmon, a civil engineer, to survey, mark and name the town site's new streets. The streets running north to south between the railroad and the edge of Old Town were named First through Sixteenth Streets. Because First Street faced the tracks, nearly everyone called it Front Street. The cross streets running parallel to Railroad Avenue were named Copper, Gold, Silver, Lead, Coal and Iron, apparently reflecting some optimism that Albuquerque would become a central shipping depot for the mining industry. South of Coal, the streets were named Huning, Hazeldine and Stover. East of the tracks, Marmon named a street Broadway because he thought any proper town ought to have a street by that name. The next streets were named Arno, for Franz Huning's son, and then Edith

A view from the northeast looking toward New Town in 1943. *Library of Congress.*

and Walter for his own children. High Street lay along gravelly hills that rose into the East Mesa. At this point, the Town Company ordered him to stop, believing the town would never reach that far. By 1881, a building boom was underway. Lyman Beecher Putney put up the first structure at First and Railroad Avenue to house his store. He had brought the building with him in panels, which he transported by flatcar. This type of building was called a "perhaps house" because it could easily be moved to another place. Putney lived in his store and slept in a hammock hung from the ceiling.

Mariano Armijo thought the town needed a good hotel, and he built the Armijo House, a three-story frame structure with a Mansard roof, on the southwest corner of Third and Railroad Avenue. Believing this eastern architecture would attract more guests, he departed from the plaza's familiar adobe buildings. The A.A. Grant building, across the street from the Armijo House, was two stories tall, with space for four stores on the first floor and an opera house on the second floor. The Grant Opera House seated one thousand people. In 1882, a new hotel, the San Felipe, was built on the corner of Fifth and Gold for a cost of $103,000. It was a three-story brick building with a forty-foot tower, a fancy roof and eighty rooms.

Quitting time at the railroad work shops. *Library of Congress.*

Before long, land that was virtually worthless before the railroad began selling for $2,000 per lot. Huning, Stover and Hazeldine, Albuquerque's first land speculators, presumably did very well. With the railroad established, Huning began building the Highland Addition between Copper and Iron Streets. Now called Huning Highland, it was Albuquerque's first residential development. Huning was already a successful Albuquerque merchant, having opened his first store in 1857. Three years after the railroad's arrival, he built a fourteen-room mansion called Castle Huning at Railroad Avenue (Central) and Fifteenth Street. (It was torn down in 1955.) The Pereas of Bernalillo might have missed an opportunity in not negotiating with the railroad, but they weren't out of the game. José L. Perea prospered in Albuquerque, building his subdivision, now called the Downtown Neighborhood District, in 1881. All of these men continued to be movers and shakers.

The railroad delivered goods in a quantity that freighters had previously hauled in on wagons and mule trains. It also expanded the city's cultural diversity. Before the railroad, Albuquerque's population was mostly Hispanic, with a small minority of Anglos. By 1885, the town consisted of more than twenty ethnic groups, including African Americans, Italians and Chinese, who built the line and decided to settle here. The town's economy soon boomed as Albuquerque became a shipping point for livestock, wool and lumber. In the early 1900s, the American Lumber Co. was second only to the railroad as the city's largest employer. Its 110-acre complex was constructed between 1903 and 1905 near Twelfth Street. At its peak, it employed 850 men and produced milled lumber, shingles and doors. Today, this area is called the Sawmill neighborhood.

By 1891, the population of Albuquerque had grown to four thousand. The town had twenty saloons and two banks, one of which went broke during the panic of 1893. The city also had as many as twenty-four gambling establishments. People were moving to Albuquerque for health reasons, and the city was taking on many aspects of larger eastern cities. Even after the 1900s, there were still occasional stage holdups, and by 1903, there had been two cases of school money embezzlement by the city's officials.

Looking northwest from the railroad. *Library of Congress.*

Looking east from the outskirts of New Town. *Library of Congress.*

In 1914, the railroad began building its maintenance shops south of New Town, along with a seventy-five-stall roundhouse, one of the railroad's largest at that time. For many years, the railroad was the city's largest employer with 1,700 workers. A steam whistle on the 240-foot smokestack of the roundhouse blew at 7:30 a.m. to start the workday and again at noon for lunch. At 4:00 p.m., it signaled quitting time.

Albuquerque got air service in 1929, but it didn't affect the railroad for decades. That year, Albuquerque was a stop on the first coast-to-coast transportation route using airplanes and trains. Airplanes then didn't fly at night, so Transcontinental Air Transport service paired with railroads. For the two-day trip from New York to Los Angeles, passengers flew during the day and traveled by train at night.

In the 1950s, the railroad began using diesel fuel instead of coal, and passengers began to do more driving. Air travel gained popularity, and there were more trucks hauling freight. As a result, the railroad started to decline. It closed its shops in the 1970s and, sadly, also tore down the Alvarado Hotel after a fire damaged it in 1993. Eventually, the Santa Fe Railway became the Burlington Northern Santa Fe Corporation after several mergers in the 1990s. Today it operates more than one thousand trains across a 33,500-mile rail system in twenty-eight states.

As Albuquerque is one of North America's oldest cities, rich in a history of conquest, conflict, religion, business and violent death, it is not surprising that it also has so many exciting ghost stories.

2
THE KIMO THEATER

Oreste Bachechi first became involved with the movies around 1919, when the Bachechi Amusement Association operated the Pastime Theatre with Joe Barnett. However, by 1925, he had decided to build his own theater, focusing on the American Indian culture of the Southwest in its architectural design. The colors took several months to choose. Like its abstract symbols, color, too, was part of the Native American vocabulary. Red is a somewhat important color because it represents the life-giving sun. White expresses the approaching morning, while yellow is representative of the setting sun of the west. Finally, the color black is symbolic of the darkening clouds from the north. The crowning touch was the seven murals painted by Carl Von Hassler. Some of the work he rendered himself; the rest was traced from heavy butcher paper cut-outs that were taped to the walls and filled in with paint by workmen. Working from a platform hung from the ceiling, Von Hassler reportedly spent months on his creations.

The theater was named the KiMo and opened in 1927. The name is a combination of two Indian words meaning "mountain lion" but more often interpreted as "king of its kind." The theater cost $150,000 and was completed in less than a year. The elaborate Wurlitzer organ that was used to accompany the silent films shown at that time was an extra $18,000.

The interior included plaster ceiling beams that were textured to look like logs and painted with dance and hunt scenes. The air vents were also disguised as Navajo rugs. The walls were decorated with panoramic murals

The KiMo Theater in 1943. *Library of Congress.*

depicting the Seven Cities of Cibola, which were accented by chandeliers shaped like war drums and Native American death canoes. However, its most prominent feature was the rows of garlanded longhorn steer skulls with eerie, glowing amber eyes.

When the theater was packed, the balcony, which spans the east to west walls without center support, was designed to give and sway. It would drop four to eight inches in the middle at peak capacity. The first movie shown in the KiMo was *Painting the Town Red*, and the first talking movie was *Melody of Broadway*. Frances Farney played the Wurlitzer organ during each performance.

The KiMo was also a significant employer for young people just getting started. Vivian Vance, who gained fame as Lucille Ball's sidekick in the *I Love Lucy* series, also worked at the KiMo. The theater hosted such Hollywood stars as Sally Rand, Gloria Swanson, Tom Mix and Ginger Rogers.

A year after the KiMo theater opened, Oreste Bachechi died, leaving the management of the KiMo to his sons. They combined vaudeville and out-of-town roadshows with movies and created extra revenue by adding a luncheonette and curio shop on either side of the entrance. In later years,

The theater in 1999 showing the changes to its signage. *Library of Congress.*

the Kiva-Hi, a second-floor restaurant, and KGGM radio were housed on the second and third floors.

On August 1, 1951, a water heater exploded during a full showing of Abbott and Costello's movie *Comin' Round the Mountain*. Several people were injured, and six-year-old Bobby Darnall was killed. Apparently, at a particularly scary part of the film, Bobby became so frightened that he ran downstairs at the exact moment a furnace exploded. He was the only one killed.

The 1960s brought hardship and financial challenges to the theater. The KiMo fell into disrepair following the exodus from downtown that so many American cities have experienced. In 1961, the screen of the theater caught fire and was heavily damaged, causing the theater to close temporarily. Two years later, the main stage was also destroyed by fire but was haphazardly rebuilt.

In December 1970, the theater finally closed. According to the *Albuquerque Journal*, the KiMo had several shifts in viewing policy—adult "art" movies, then Spanish, before returning to Spanish-English. However, by October 1972, the KiMo was active and running plays. A review of the play *The Amorous Flea* ran in the *Albuquerque Journal*; however, the downtown area was abandoned for uptown shopping centers and twin-screen movie houses. The theater struggled to survive. The final blow came in November 1974 when the Madowhy Corp and the Mature Pictures Corp filed charges against the Commonwealth theaters, who were operating the KiMo, accusing that the KiMo was showing a bogus, unauthorized and illegal copy of the film *The Life and Times of the Happy Hooker*. The suit sought a permanent injunction and $75,000 in damages. By 1975, the old theater was slated for demolition. Within a year, the city of Albuquerque was interested in buying the theater in hopes of repairing it as a part of the revitalization of the downtown area. The *Albuquerque Journal* ran a short story on September 30, 1976, that reads: "The City Spirit group said the KiMo is no longer usable as a modern movie theater but might be restored and used for performing arts. In addition to the theater, which remains closed, the building contains two small retail stores and several offices."

The KiMo was eventually saved in 1977 when the citizens of Albuquerque voted to purchase this historic theater. The voters rejected the second bond to provide matching funds to a federal grant, so the City of Albuquerque allocated $1.1 million for a partial renovation. Everyone was excited about the theater's reclamation.

Architects Harvey Hoshour and Dan Pearson started the first phase of the renovation. The buffalo skulls were repainted to their original colors, and old photographs were used to replicate the mission light fixtures on the façade. The Kachina door handles were also duplicated from the one remaining handle that was left at the theater. The balcony railing in the lobby was too short to meet modern safety codes, so Hoshour had additional metal inserted in the birds' necks and legs to make the decorative railing eleven inches taller. Another restoration phase focused solely on the Carl Von Hassler murals and would end up costing $35,000.

The second phase of renovation was not started until the spring of 1999 and was completed in the summer of 2000. The original proscenium arch that was destroyed in a 1960s fire was replicated, and new stage lighting positions were also created. The original grand drape also had to be reproduced and included several unique features, including medallions and several hand-painted details.

The entire ceiling in the auditorium was carefully cleaned, repaired and restored. Chandeliers modeled after Native American funerary canoes were hung above the audience, and vigas (roof beams) were painted and adorned with Pueblo Indian motifs.

During the removal of the old acoustic materials applied to the walls, the original artwork was discovered underneath. The art depicted Navajo Yei

The theater in 2020, closed due to the coronavirus pandemic. *Photo by author.*

The ticket booth of the theater with its elaborate decorations. *Library of Congress.*

figures and sandpaintings, but they were too damaged to be repaired. The images were carefully photographed and replicated by art conservationists on the new acoustic wall fabric. New carpet and flooring were installed throughout the theater, and the auditorium seating was entirely replaced to meet modern building and accessibility codes.

Electrical upgrades, a more modern control booth and a new stage-level dressing room were also completed. The KiMo's second-floor business offices were renovated over the winter of 2000, and the third-floor office area was renovated in 2002. Both floors had upgraded plumbing and electrical systems as well as new roofing.

Today, the ghost of Bobby Darnall is said to haunt the KiMo theater. It is believed that Bobby is prone to playing tricks and pranks on the crew if they do not appease him by bribing him with doughnuts or other trinkets, leaving them out before performances so that he won't interfere with the show.

The dozens of ghost stories at the KiMo theater provide a proliferating amount of information that makes it challenging to sort out. The easiest way to make sense of it is to take a sampling of the stories that have been presented in ascending chronological order.

The first printed article about the KiMo Theater's ghost appears in the *Albuquerque Journal* on July 10, 1988. Written by Carole Mazur, it appears in the theater section of the paper. Written only seven months after the performance of *A Christmas Carol*, the article contains several critical clues about the ghost story and reads as follows:

> *Thirteen donuts hang from pipes on the back wall of the KiMo Theatre this month, the past year's peace offerings to a child-like ghost with a sweet tooth and a talent for computer hacking.*
>
> *Things go wrong in mysterious ways whenever anyone removes the little round talismans, insists Tony Marsh, the KiMo's technical director. Along the dark-red brick wall at the rear of the stage, the 13 donuts, one of them chocolate, dangle on ribbons or strings at irregular intervals. Two tortillas, one corn, and one flour add Southwestern flavor to the collection.*
>
> *The hanging of the donuts started three seasons ago, Marsh recalls.*
>
> *In the fall of 1985, the crew foreman of Opera Southwest brought a box of doughnuts and coffee for his technical crew each morning. When they left at night, there would always be one or two doughnuts left in the box. But the following morning, the doughnuts would be gone.*
>
> *"Now I would be the first one here and the last one to leave, and I didn't take them," says the slender Marsh. "But the doughnuts would be gone.*

So as a lark, crew members started tying doughnuts against the back wall. Eventually, there were six or seven doughnuts up there, and nobody really thought anything about it."

The next chapter came in December 1986, when the New Mexico Repertory Theatre moved in to set up "A Christmas Carol." Since the Victorian set design called for a bareback wall, the Rep's crew removed the crumby decorations.

"The night of the Tech rehearsal before the first performance, everything that could go wrong went wrong," Marsh remembers. "Light cues didn't work. Sound cues didn't work. Actors were walking into each other. It was a total disaster."

The Rep stage manager placed some doughnuts backstage the next morning, and the preview night went like clockwork.

"It became a ritual with the Rep that whenever they moved in, they would hang a doughnut on the wall," Marsh says, "and everything was great. But then the opera quit bringing doughnuts, and the same thing happened to them."

These days Marsh can't remember the production's name, but the chaotic rehearsal remains vivid.

"It's always the same thing," he says, "nothing goes right technically."

The many computerized light and sound cues the crew spent many hours running and re-running without a hitch would suddenly malfunction for no discernible reason. Then the next day, the computer program would run perfectly again without any readjustments.

"Now, whenever something goes wrong," Marsh adds, "somebody says, 'It's time for a doughnut.' If nothing else, it gives people time to calm down. Minor mishaps occasionally occur even with the doughnuts on duty," he says. "But it's mainly human error, things that you can explain away."

Some people believe the calamities are the work of the ghost of a child killed in the theater, Marsh says.

On Aug. 2, 1951, 6-year old Bobby Darnall was killed when a hot water heater exploded in the lobby. Bobby and two friends, Lou Ellen and Ronald Ross, were in the balcony for a matinee of Abbott and Costello's "Comin' Round the Mountain" when Bobby startled, apparently at a noise in the movie, and started running down the stairway to the lobby. He headed straight into the blast.

Ronald Ross, now an Albuquerque attorney, said in a telephone interview that no one ever figured out exactly why Bobby left his seat. (Attempts to contact the Darnall family were unsuccessful.)

Marsh says that he has occasionally heard a door closing or the sound of whispering when he has been alone in the theater.

"I haven't actually seen a materialization," he says while gazing towards the balcony, "but I have heard things that were kind of strange. And this is a pretty spooky building when you're all by yourself at 2 in the morning."

"Theater people are a superstitious bunch," says Marsh, "so nearly all the Albuquerque performing groups who use the KiMo now contribute at least one doughnut per production to the back wall's decor. If an old doughnut happens to crumble and fall, the group will immediately replace it, even if it means working shorthanded while someone races to the nearest doughnut shop right before a performance."

Out-of-town groups playing one night stands usually come unprepared for the KiMo tradition. But once they find out about it, they don't want the doughnuts taken down, Marsh says.

"Sometimes there are doughnuts all over the place," Marsh says, estimating that he throws away about 50 during the season. "They're in the dressing rooms, the prop shop, the boiler room. But I try to draw the line because on the stage wall is where they belong."

At the end of July, Marsh removes all the doughnuts to make room for new ones in the upcoming season.

"That's the way we officially signify the end of the year," he says. "We're closed in August to do repairs. We've never done a show right after I've taken the doughnuts down. I'd be curious to see what happens."

But then Marsh adds, with a nervous laugh, "If a major show suddenly got booked, I would probably go out and get some doughnuts myself, because I know it works, and I'd just as soon not mess with it."

Over the next decade, there were more stories published, but the story underwent several distinct changes. In March 2004, an article ran in the *Weekly Alibi*, an alternative weekly newspaper in Albuquerque. The article was written by Stephanie Garcia and Tim McGivern and described the KiMo ghost story as it existed at that time. The article is called "Is There Something Weird in the Neighborhood?" The changes in the story are quite apparent when you compare it with the 1988 article. It reads:

The KiMo Theatre, a Downtown architectural jewel and historic landmark, in Tewa, means "king of its kind." Its multi-million dollar renovation has made it one of the fanciest and most intimate places to enjoy the arts and, some say, maybe even do a little ghost-spotting.

The stage of the KiMo Theater. *Wikimedia Commons.*

Dennis Potter, the theater's technical stage manager, sincerely said there was a ghost who lived there as he pointed out the KiMo's architectural design during a recent tour of the place.

On Aug. 1, 1951, the theatre's water heater exploded in the lobby during a show. "It was very gruesome," Potter said. "One little boy named Bobby Darnall was critically injured and died."

Potter led the way to a shrine in the back of the building that is dedicated to Darnall, who was six years old when he died. The shrine contained many little items such as beads, fake flowers, small toys, and pictures. Potter said some people place things there for the ghost in hopes that the show will go well and added that certain occurrences happened to make them believe that the paranormal talk wasn't just an old wives' tale. One of them was during a showing of Charles Dickens' A Christmas Carol. "Everything went wrong," Potter said, "light bulbs were exploding, and doors were opening and closing by themselves." On another night, one ticket lady allegedly saw a boy standing on the balcony when everyone else had left the building.

Another instance was when the third floor was under renovation. Business renters from across the street said that they saw a small boy smiling and waving from the third floor. Overall, Potter said the ghost is pretty peaceful.

Craig Rivera, the manager of the KiMo, is not exactly convinced that the ghost really exists. "I have never seen, sensed, felt, or tasted anything," Rivera said. "Maybe I've become immune. Do I think it's possible? Maybe so." Rivera said a few KiMo visitors have been freaked out because they felt a presence.

A 1951 issue of the Albuquerque Journal *featured the explosion on the front page, accompanied by a picture of Darnall, who was a light-haired, fair-skinned child from what you can make out in the grainy image. The KiMo staff still has an original copy of the issue as part of the theater archives.*

Rivera said that there are not a lot of records of the KiMo during those times. "In 1951, the KiMo was privately owned and operated; all the records are gone. Who knows what could have taken place?"

Rivera said that this ghost talk has caused all kinds of curiosity among the public. "We get calls from all ghostbuster types of groups to see if they can channel some energy. I've had people who come in here and can feel the energy." He added that several people wanted to do documentaries of the ghost.

Due to and despite the speculation of a phantom, the theater continues to be a significant part of Albuquerque's history and culture. Rivera said that it's all up to the person as to whether they believe. "Let your own mind and your own instincts be the judge."

What has actually happened is quite common among ghost stories. Over the years, various incidents have been lumped together by various storytellers as the tale passed from one person to the next. The end result is a process called myth-building. It is a fusion of various tales that were blended together to make the story more manageable and more dramatic to tell. In the process, it also conceals the original tale behind the new version of the story, obscuring facts and details.

A local actress named Cathy told me an interesting story of a ghostly incident that had occurred at the theater. She was a member of a local acting group performing a play on Hispanic culture at the KiMo. When she arrived for rehearsals, no one in the group knew of the tradition of leaving Bobby his due. During the next several weeks, the play was fine-tuned, and finally, they were ready for opening night. That was when things got interesting. The props were stored on stage left; however, when the time came to use one of them, the props had mysteriously disappeared. A brief search of the area by the staff backstage revealed that the props had somehow been moved over to stage right. That side of the stage can only be accessed by going down a basement corridor, passing the dressing rooms and other occupied spaces. Yet no one was able to explain how the props were moved from one side to the other.

Regarding it as a simple curiosity, they finished their performance and thought nothing else of the ordeal. The following night, the same incident happened again. The props, on stage left, had once again been moved back over to the right side of the stage, undetected by any of the actors or staff. Finally, the acting group learned of Bobby, and later that night, after the performance, they made a late-night trip to Walmart to buy assorted goodies for the boy's spirit.

After placing the items near the old steam pipe, the production had no further problems. Bobby has also been seen playing on the stairs leading to the balcony. He is described as having brown hair and wearing a striped shirt and jeans.

Because the incident was recent, I was able to question other people who were involved in the performance. This particular event did have a rational explanation. The stage manager was aware of the moving props because he ordered the props to be moved. Several scenes had entries and exits on stage left, and he felt that the props could become a tripping hazard. So, the stage crew moved them.

Cathy, who is admittedly a believer in the paranormal, jumped to a conclusion about the moved props after learning about the ghostly boy's story. It did not occur to her to seek an alternative explanation for the event. As I continued to sort through the other reported encounters, I discovered that they all had other possible explanations that were completely logical.

Figuring out how the ghost story started involves the investigation of two clues. The first revolves around a simple question. How did the crew know that replacing a donut would calm down the spirit of the little boy? This indicates that the superstition was already in existence before the performance of *A Christmas Carol*. Thus, to find the beginning of the ghost tradition, one must look further into the past.

The second clue can be found in the accounts of the people who have claimed to have had a ghostly encounter. In the beginning, it manifested to the technical crew as computer glitches, causing malfunctions in the lighting and sound. Once the first story about the theater was published, the majority of the ghostly encounters involved the theater staff or the production crew and actors. This usually occurred when the ghost of Bobby had not left some sort of offering. However, there is one deviation from this pattern. It is the story of a young boy waving at people from the third-floor window while the building was under construction. From the theater's history, it is known that there was construction on the third floor in 2002. I suspect that this might be the incident that Craig Rivera referred to in the television show *Weird Travels*. However, the story of a boy being seen in the window predates 2002. It was known by many of the theater's staff and some of the local actors. I suspected that this might be the genesis of the ghost stories.

The ghost stories of the KiMo Theater appear to be nothing more than an urban legend. Urban legends typically include one or more common elements, in this case, the phenomenon surrounding the doughnuts, and the legend is retold on behalf of the original witness or participant (Tony Marsh).

The legend starts with a suggestion that the building has a ghost of a little boy who was seen in the third-floor window after the city had purchased the building. Since the building had been an adult theater, it caused an alarm when people walking on the street saw a boy in one of the windows. Concerned, they called the police.

According to the ghost story, once the police arrived, the building was found to be empty. However, there were children in the building that day. An article in the *Albuquerque Journal* (April 27, 1977) states that "volunteers from Albuquerque Boys Club, Rio Grande High School, and the Downtown Exchange Club wiped into every nook and cranny as the dusty seats and faded carpets began to reveal some of their former luster."

So, the catalyst for the ghost story was created with the suggestion that a little boy is haunting the theater. Eventually, the doughnut tradition started, as a lark, in 1985. The association of little bite marks in the doughnuts is a product of myth-building. However, it is still used as a point of validity for the phenomenon being linked to the ghostly boy.

Then, during a tech rehearsal for the play *A Christmas Carol* in 1987, the doughnut tradition was linked to the suggestion that the theater is haunted by a child who was then only known as the "hungry little ghost." The initially reported phenomenon consisted solely of malfunctioning technical effects. Sound and light cues did not work, and actors were bumping into each other.

Within the next seven months, the ghost was "identified" as Bobby Darnall, a child who was tragically killed in 1951. By 1988, the *Albuquerque Journal* had published the first account of the events that happened at the KiMo. The myth-building started. The theater began propagating the myth by establishing a "shrine" to its resident spirit and producing/distributing literature containing the ghost story. The phenomenon, driven by the witnesses' confirmation bias, now focused on the "experiences"

Bobby's shrine, where offerings are left for the theater's ghost. *Photo by author.*

of the actors and visitors. The technical issues of the first event were forgotten as guests and visitors were biased by the ghost story and started misinterpreting ordinary events as paranormal-oriented ones. They also began noticing things that were not seen previously and, as a result, wrongly assumed that this newly discovered phenomenon was paranormal in origin. This drove the myth by creating an illusion of validity that was vital to the ghost story's longevity.

SEVERAL OTHER SPIRITS ARE also believed to roam about the theater as well. A woman dressed in "Old West" attire has been spotted in the hallway leading to the bathrooms and on the balcony itself.

Witnesses describe her dress as being composed of a gingham pattern with a bustle, with a bonnet on the apparition's head. The ghost is said to be about five feet tall and solid, not glowing or transparent as one might expect. Her appearances are always very brief, no more than a few seconds at most. Another ghost seen on the balcony is that of a well-dressed gentleman. Wearing a black suit and top hat, he is only seen during performances and seems to prefer the left side of the balcony, as viewed from the stage. He always vanishes midway through the play or production. Both the ghosts of the woman and man are unidentified. However, it appears that these particular specters have been forgotten by the staff today and are seldom talked about.

3
THE WOOL WAREHOUSE THEATER

By 1917, Frank Bond was a prominent man in New Mexico business, owning twelve companies in the state. Española was the headquarters for all of the Bond Interests. In 1924 and 1928, he was a possible gubernatorial candidate. However, Bond insisted that his good friend Richard C. Dillon, who was also Republican, run for governor. Dillon won the election. Although Bond never ran for governor, he remained politically active in Española with the Republican Party. He then pushed for the incorporation of Española into a municipality, and after succeeding in doing that, he helped elect the first mayor, F.R. Frankenburger. Frank also served as "popular" mayor of Española from 1907 to 1913 and again from 1918 to 1922. He was also a trustee on the local school board in Española.

When Frank Bond moved his headquarters to Albuquerque in 1925, he did so not only to be in the market center of the wool industry in the Southwest but also because of his daughter Hazel's health. Hazel had contracted tuberculosis, and Albuquerque was known for its multiple treatment centers. Tragically, it was his other daughter, Amy, who died suddenly in the following year. As if this was not enough, Hazel died two years later. In the same year as Hazel's death, work on the Wool Warehouse was begun. Perhaps these two tragic losses so close to one another motivated him to start work on this new project. After his daughters' deaths, Bond decided to stay in Albuquerque, where he purchased a large home. He moved most of his wool businesses to Albuquerque and established a few more business ventures. He built the Wool Warehouse Company with his son, Frank Bond Jr., and several other partners.

The Wool Warehouse Theater. *Photo by author.*

By 1930, the warehouse had taken its first clip of wool and continued as a center for wool and hide sales and storage until 1972, when the sharp decline in wool production caused the Bonds to lease the building to other tenants. They continued to own the building until 1976, when they sold it to the City of Albuquerque, which used it for record storage.

The Wool Warehouse was eventually declared a National Historic Landmark in 1978. Designed in 1928 by T. Charles Gaastra, the Monte Vista and Eugene Field Elementary Schools architect, the Wool Warehouse is a two-story, forty-thousand-square-foot brick building. Built in 1929, the building housed offices of the New Mexico Cooperative Wool Marketing Association, Bond McRae Company (dealers in wool) and the New Mexico–Arizona Wool Warehouse Company.

Frank Bond in 1903. *Center for Southwest Research, University Libraries, University of New Mexico–UNM Digital Libraries.*

The Wool Warehouse is a two-story, elongated brick cube that measures one hundred by two hundred feet. It is an exceptionally strong building because it has a concrete skeleton with double brick infill walls ranging from eight inches to two feet. The wider wall widths enabled the interior sliding doors to clear the two-foot columns of the skeleton while retaining the flush appearance of the exterior wall. The structural skeleton of the building is concealed on all sides by multiple courses of raked brick. A three-foot concrete wall anchors everything to the base of the exterior.

Located between the railroad tracks and First Street in downtown Albuquerque, the building's only ornamented wall is its public façade on First Street, which faces the west. On this wall, denoted by projecting brickwork, is a vehicle entrance flanked by concrete columns. The corner bays extend one foot from the façade. The exterior is accentuated further by projecting vertical courses of bricks, forming a two-story frame around the first- and second-story windows. Paired concrete vertical ornaments were placed on either side of the second-story windows flanking the vehicle entrance. The concrete ornamentation blends in with the continuous, smooth concrete coping that wraps around the top of the entire building. The roof is flat except for a one-story brick "penthouse" on the east end, which houses the upper terminal of a large freight elevator.

The interior is very straightforward. It consists of two substantial storage rooms that are stacked on top of one another. The rooms are supported by four rows of nine concrete columns that extend across the length of the building. The columns are sixteen feet, eight inches tall. They are topped by flared fluted capitals that suggest that the building's designer had an Egyptian temple in mind when he designed this post and beam warehouse. The ample interior space is interrupted only by a small group of offices in the northwest corner and a concrete stairway. Toward the southeast are two small concrete rooms. One was used to store salt bins and the other contained brine vats. A ten-by-eighteen-foot freight elevator was centered on the rear (east) wall, and a curving, steel spiral staircase once

The original safe is still inside the old building. *Photo by author.*

stood just east of the front offices. A steel dog-leg stair eventually replaced this staircase. Metal pipe openings, four inches in diameter, are set in the floors and ceilings of both stories. These once held the narrower floor-to-ceiling metal pipes to which racks were attached. The racks were used to hang thousands of skins and hides during curing and storage.

In 1982, the firm of Mitchell/McClure architects created detailed plans to remodel the building. It was completely renovated in 1985 by the architectural/planning firm of Boehning, Protz, Cook, and Associates at the cost of $2.5 million. The firm was given the 1985 Honor Award for renovating the former wool processing plant into the Wool Warehouse Theater and Restaurant.

The interior of the Wool Warehouse reflected an Art Deco adaptation of the Egyptian-style columns that are part of the original 1926 structure. David Cook was the project and design architect. This project transformed a 1929 monument to New Mexico's role in the wool industry.

In 1984, it was leased by Betty and George Luce, who turned the second floor into a theater restaurant. It was still a classy place, perfect for an upscale dinner theater, as it "recalls an era of casual elegance" with "massive columns featuring Egyptian motifs and Roaring Twenties Art Deco appointments." This building became the Wool Warehouse Theater Restaurant. It encompasses five thousand square feet and holds up to 350 people, 250 for dinner theater.

To accommodate the theater, a substantial portion of the roof structure was removed. This allowed a full-height proscenium opening with a fly loft to be constructed. In 2004, the Wool Warehouse Theater Restaurant building was bought by Double Tree Hotels.

On June 21, 1945, Frank Bond died in Los Angeles, California, due to chronic heart alignment. His sole heir was his son, Frank Jr., who took over as president of Frank Bond & Son. He also ran the other companies and held the vast family interests until 1953, when he died unexpectedly from a sudden illness. With no other family members able to manage operations, the business partners began selling off its assets, and the empire that Bond had built was liquidated. Bond is buried at the Fairview Memorial Cemetery in Albuquerque, along with other family members.

Since 1994, the Wool Warehouse Theater has been owned and operated by Youth Development Inc., a local nonprofit, and has been used sporadically for concerts, dances and other events.

Today, it is believed that Frank Bond haunts the old building. His apparition is rumored to have been seen in the theater, talking to the women in the audience before he mysteriously vanishes. Yet another ghost, possibly his wife, disapproves of Frank's flirtatious behavior and locks women in the bathroom.

The first reported occurrence happened in 1985. There are a few variants, but the basic story goes like this:

> *During the first production presented in the theater, the Stage Manager, Vicki, kept seeing a cream-colored thing go past her. Then at intermission, she went to check something on the left side of the stage. Then suddenly, she saw the apparition of an immaculate, charming looking man who was wearing a cream-colored, double-breasted suit. He was standing right next to the prop table, happily watching what was going on. According to Vicki, he appeared to be very pleased with the theater production.*
>
> *In the following years, employees and guests have felt hot and cold spots and have felt a presence among them, watching them. Things and objects in the theater have gone missing, only to reappear in other places in the building. Employees avoided going down the stairs behind the stage area to the basement unless they had to go there. It was reported that employees have felt a push from unseen hands while attempting to go down the stairs and had something grab at their ankles. Strange sounds have been heard coming from the walls as well. Cold spots and an eerie presence have also been felt by customers and employees.*

An actress, Lisa, who has participated in previous productions at the theater, has had several encounters with the spirit that roams about the historic building. She spoke to me about one encounter that had a profound effect on her:

> *During several of the rehearsals, I had many different and unusual experiences. There is a hallway of sorts that runs behind the stage area that simply has a creepy feel about it. It feels as if someone is always there and that you are being watched. One time, when I was walking back there, I felt a hand grab my shoulder as if someone was trying to stop me. I felt this large hand holding tightly onto me. Assuming that it was one of the other performers, I turned around to see who it was. There was no one there, yet I still could feel the pressure of a hand squeezing my shoulder. This sensation disappeared as my name was called by another one of the actresses. I quickly ran out of the hallway and back around to the stage.*

It seems that the majority of Lisa's experiences have occurred in the same area. She often felt something brushing against her face. Most of the time, she assumed that it was merely a spider web, and other than wondering where the spider was, she did not give it much thought. That quickly changed one evening when she once again felt the unusual sensation of something brushing against her, except on this occasion, she began to see strands of her hair being lifted up into the air as if an invisible hand was caressing her face and playing with her hair. This happened several times, but she would simply shake her head and go on about her business. Lisa speculates that perhaps she resembles the spirit's wife somehow, and although her experiences were startling, she claims that she was never terrified of the ghost itself.

Another actor, Chris, has been involved in several productions at the old theater. At the first two rehearsals, he felt a freezing gust of air moving past him and often felt the presence of someone else other than his fellow actors. Being a little skeptical, he ignored the cold spots of air, believing them to be nothing more than drafts. He had heard the stories of the building being haunted but thought that the ghost stories were nothing but nonsense. After all, old buildings like this one seem to have a character that some might consider spooky. His opinion was swiftly changed one evening when he heard a man shout at him from a darkened corner of the stage. Although he was startled by this experience, he managed to get a good look at the ghost. It was an older man with gray hair wearing a double-breasted, cream-colored suit. The ghost soon disappeared, right before his eyes. After that experience, Chris refused to go to the theater again.

The women's restroom has also seen occasional bouts of ghostly activity. One employee heard the sound of a woman screaming coming from inside the restroom. After trying for several minutes to open the door, he finally kicked the door in, only to find the restroom empty. There have also been reports of women who have been stuck in the restroom. Although the door is unlocked, it seems to be held closed by an unseen force just outside.

One waitress tried to get out for fifteen minutes, yelling for help and pushing on the door before it finally opened by itself. Other women, including guests, have also reported similar experiences.

The unidentified ghost of a man in a double-breasted, cream-colored suit has appeared near the stage during performances, thought to be one of the men in the Bond family. The figure is believed to be Frank Bond himself.

Unlike many of the haunted places that I have mentioned in this book, I have not been able to locate any newspaper articles that have suggested that the theater is haunted or any ghost stories coming from the Wool

The lobby of the theater/restaurant. *Photo by author.*

Warehouse. However, in the early 1990s, the building was also used as a Halloween haunted attraction called the First Street Morgue, and in 1996, the haunted house was called Screamworks. A friend of mine, Carl, told me of his experiences there:

> *It was October 6th, 1993. I was at a concert somewhere and met up with a friend working at the First Street Morgue, a haunted house attraction. This was also before the renovation in the upstairs theater.*
>
> *So, my friend told me, "Hey, you like* Friday the 13th *so much, why don't you come down and try out to play Jason?"*
>
> *So, I did. At first, the manager, Gino, didn't want to hire me because I didn't have a full Jason outfit. So, I told him I'd get one that night and agreed to work the night for free so he could see how many customers I could scare. Fortunately, he agreed, and I came back with an excellent Jason set up with a real hockey mask, not a cheap imitation.*
>
> *I showed up, got dressed and scared more people than any other actor! Gino was impressed, and before he said I got the gig, I told him that I had*

so much fun that I would do it for half the pay. I was only seventeen years old and still living at home, so money wasn't that high on my list.

The next day, I arrived at 5:00 p.m., ready to scare more people. Gino and his wife, Kim, introduced me to the crew and told me the rules. The main rule was not to go into the theater under any circumstances. I was told this was due to the historic nature of that part of the building. Now I'm a seventeen-year-old metalhead kid whose new job is playing Jason from my favorite movie series, and I had no appreciation for authority. At that time, I had respect for it but only when I wanted to.

A couple of nights went by, and we got busier the closer it got to Halloween. However, my "experience" didn't happen on Halloween. It happened the weekend before the 24th or 25th. Someone had booked a rave, so now we had a loud techno light show in the setting of a haunted house. Needless to say, it killed the mood for the haunted house.

They had an industrial movie fog machine mixing with our fog machines at about 10:30 p.m.; the place was getting so thick with smoke, we turned off ours. By 11:00 p.m., I couldn't take anymore. The fog, smoke, temperature and weight of my costume was too much to bear anymore.

I asked Gino for the keys upstairs so that I could get out of costume and take a half-hour break. He gave me the keys and said to lock it behind me because he didn't want any ravers to get upstairs. Doing this would lock me out of the area, but his wife had the other key, and she would come by in half an hour to let me back in.

So, after going back out, I locked the door as requested and headed up the stairs. I'm halfway up when I heard footsteps on the other side of the dividing wall, which led into the theater. I immediately thought that some ravers were up here. I gripped my machete tight and said to myself, "I'll scare them out of here!"

If they were heading to the stage area by going through the right entrance, I could intercept them by entering stage left. Quickly, I passed the dressing rooms and ran to the back hall into the stage left entrance. I didn't hear any voices, so I thought there must only be one or two of them. Knowing that I had them cornered, I busted out of stage left, but no one was there.

Then in full Jason style, I stalked the stage but still found no one. I started looking into the seats, then the balcony, still nothing. Then I thought they might have gone to the kitchen, but all of the lights were off except for the stage. I didn't see flashlights moving about, so I listened and waited to see if they made any noises or bumped into something.

I hung out for several minutes before deciding to give up. I wanted to have a smoke and a coke before I had to go back to work. As I turned to leave, I saw this old man, perhaps in his late forties or early fifties, on the balcony. I could only see part of his right side, half his head, and most of his torso. I could also make out what appeared to be the outline of his hat.

The figure was sitting there, and he looked like he was clapping his hands, but there was no sound at all. Just as I start to focus on him, he was gone. I ran to stage right to get to the hall, then to the lobby, to get to the balcony steps. However, the area was empty. No one was there. I ran back down the stairs to the door, which was still locked, and waited until I was let back inside.

At the end of the night, I described the "old dude" I saw to Gino. I described him as an older guy wearing a brownish suit with a vest and jacket. He wore an old-school hat and had facial hair, but the mustache was thicker than everything else. It reminded me of the older hairstyles that men wore back in the 1920s. Gino said no one there that night looked even close to that, then I told him the story of chasing the ravers and seeing him. Gino said that's one of the reasons why we couldn't go into the theater. The leasing guy told Gino that a couple of people saw and heard things they can't explain.

The original signage of the business still exists on its east side. *Wikimedia Commons.*

> *I worked the warehouse again in '96, but the whole upstairs was renovated and blocked off. No one could get up. Eventually, I ended up being a DJ at the Icehouse, which is connected to the warehouse. The Icehouse was the cold storage for the wool, and in the office, you can hear all kinds of stuff located in the basement of the actual club.*

Several books mention the haunting of the Wool Warehouse; however, they contain the same basic information that I have already provided.

The one real mystery find was why the entrance to the penthouse, the terminal of the freight elevator, had been sealed off. It seems that might have been some usable space for props or other supplies for the theater.

The Wool Warehouse Theater is a popular venue for weddings and other types of productions. If the building was haunted, there should be significantly more witness accounts and the descriptions of its apparition would be somewhat consistent. The phenomenon that people have described as paranormal was investigated and found to have several alternative explanations. I do not believe that there is a probable rationality to believe that this location is haunted, but it does make a suitable ghost story.

4
The Hotel Andaluz

New Mexico native Conrad Hilton, who honeymooned in Albuquerque with bride Zsa Zsa Gabor, built La Posada de Albuquerque in 1939. This ten-story hotel is listed in the National Register of Historic Places.

The hotel opened on June 9, 1939, and was the fourth hotel Hilton managed. Because Hilton was a native of New Mexico, it was only appropriate to build this grand hotel in the bustling city of Albuquerque, across from the railroad station. Although this was the third property he had purchased, it was his first in the Land of Enchantment. The hotel went through some rough times and was even vacant for a while, but it has recently been refurbished and claims its original grandeur. It was named La Posada, which means "the resting place."

Handcrafted wood railings encompass the balcony that overlooks the two-story lobby. An elaborate Moorish brass-and-mosaic fountain stands in the center of the tiled lobby floor, while carpet, drapes and furniture, added in 1997, set off touches such as old-fashioned tin chandeliers hanging from the two-story ceiling. The lobby is surrounded by high archways, creating the feel of a nineteenth-century hacienda courtyard.

The Lobby Bar, with its hand-painted murals, hand-carved beams and balconies, has long been one of the city's most popular meeting spots. This lobby is a landmark in its own right.

Today, the sixty-year-old key box is still in use behind the front desk, just as it was when Thomas O. Jones (a security chief for the Manhattan Project who was responsible for evacuating the area, should the Trinity

The Hotel Andaluz. *Photo by author.*

Experiment get out of hand) watched from his fourth-floor room as the flash of the first atomic bomb exploded 110 miles away on July 16, 1945. Just a month before, atomic spy Harry Gold had signed a hotel registration card that became a key piece of evidence leading to the execution of Ethel and Julius Rosenberg.

The ballroom hosted both Senator John F. Kennedy in 1957 and Vice President Al Gore in 1998. The original carved white oak elevator panels are displayed in the north entry hall. The 1939 map in the north entry hall includes San Antonio, where patrons of the Owl Café now use the bar from the Hilton family bed-and-breakfast.

In 1969, the hotel was sold, and after a brief renovation, it became the Hotel Plaza. For the next twelve years, it was a predominant business on Route 66, until it too closed in 1981. The building was soon bought, and its name was changed again to the Hotel Bradford. However, the hotel sat vacant for three years before it was finally renovated in 1984, under the name La Posada de Albuquerque. It was under this name that the ghost stories started circulating about the hotel.

Throughout its history, the hotel witnessed many murders, which added a convenient backstory to many of its supposed ghost stories. The most brutal involved a waiter at a restaurant located in the hotel. He was murdered on the seventh floor. When the hotel maid came to clean his room one morning, she found him lying in blood, face down on the bed. Investigating police found that he had been stabbed more than thirty-five times all over his body, his spinal cord and throat cut and his head scalped. Coincidently, the seventh floor is the hotbed of many of the paranormal encounters that have been reported by guests. Its dark past presents the catalyst and suggestion needed for a ghost story to evolve.

In 2005, the hotel was sold and renovated again, eventually opening under its current name, Hotel Andaluz, in 2009. It is essential to note the long periods when the building was closed for renovations. It will play a significant part in the ghost stories later on.

Local legends say that the hotel also has its unseen visitors and occupants. A housewife, who stayed at the hotel for a week with her husband while attending a business conference, experienced one typical encounter:

> *We were staying in the La Posada Hotel located on Central Street in the downtown area. While my husband was away at various business functions, I went out on my own to shop around the many stores located on Nob Hill. I made sure I was back to the hotel room around 5 or 5:30 p.m.*

The Hilton hotel in 1943. *Library of Congress.*

so I could be there when he got home. This one particular day, I came back a little early to relax and enjoy a cup of tea in the room before going out to dinner with my husband.

I was reading the paper, and I also had CNN on the TV to catch up on the news. I was happily sipping my tea when my eyes caught the movement of a lady in a fancy dress and hat that was reminiscent of something someone would wear in the 1940s, before the start of the war. She walked away from the vanity and into the bathroom. I was quite surprised to see this because I didn't see anyone in the room when I came in, and I'm sure I would have heard someone knock at the door.

At first, I thought it might have been someone from housekeeping turning down the room for the night. But dressed up in this type of garb? I think not. I wasn't afraid.

I think I was more curious than frightened at this point. I didn't see anyone in the bathroom at all. It was just a ghost in a stunning dress and hat. I didn't see her after that incident.

Another guest had a startling experience with the hotel's ghosts in a room on the seventh floor:

One night, while I was in the bathroom, I saw an apparition of just a face. There was no physical body, just a face. I saw it in the shower as I went into the bathroom. It scared me to death at the time, and I thought it couldn't be real, so I simply assured myself that it was my imagination. My second encounter occurred later that evening, around 11:00 p.m. I was lying in bed and about to fall asleep when I had an unusual feeling that I was not alone in the room. I lifted my head and glanced over toward the bathroom door. That was when I saw her.

It was the figure of a woman wearing her pink gown. I watched in horror as she glided toward me. At first, I sat up in the bed, thinking that someone had mangled in to enter our room by mistake. As she approached the bed, her arms raised as if she was going to grab me. Then her mouth dropped open, and the most awful, horrific moan came out of her.

It was so ugly and evil, and it looked as if someone was holding up a dead body, and its jaw dropped open. I screamed and woke my boyfriend, who saw nothing, and promptly rolled back over and went to sleep. I went under the covers, and eventually, the vision faded, but the moaning continued until it dissolved into this really mirthful, tinkling laughter. I also tried very hard to pretend that the whole incident had been a dream.

Why was I the only one to see it? Well, that's my real-life encounter with a ghost.

This particular story fits the traits of old hag syndrome, otherwise known as sleep paralysis. This manifests as hallucinations that happen while you are falling asleep or as you're waking up. However, other experiences at the hotel are more challenging to define.

The central lobby of the hotel. *Photo by author.*

Another strange sighting took place in 1980 when a maid saw a beautiful girl walking near the ballroom on a rainy morning. The girl was soaking wet and appeared as if she had been crying, so the maid asked if she was OK. The girl paused and looked at her before walking into the ballroom. The maid followed and was shocked when she entered the ballroom to find it empty. She was sure that she could not have crossed the room to another exit quickly and was even more surprised to see no wet footprints on the dry dance floor.

Another interesting ghost story takes place just outside of the hotel. One evening, a young girl climbed aboard the city bus and walked right past the driver without paying the fare. Oblivious to the world around her, she walked to the back portion of the vehicle and sat down. The irritated driver called out to her, telling her that she needed to pay, but the mysterious girl didn't answer. Finally, he stood up and walked to confront her. She would either pay the fare, or he would have to kick her off the bus. However, before he could reach her, she vanished right before his eyes.

One of the interesting things about the hotel is that some of its stories come from reviews on travel sites. The following is an interesting one from Trip Advisor:

I stayed at the Hotel Andaluz in January 2013 while on a business trip. My co-worker and I had rooms on different floors. Both of us didn't have the best views, but the hotel was nice and charming. We found the lobby bar to be especially unique with great character. However, one night I awoke to a very strange force or puff of wind in my face. I woke up from this and was immediately unnerved. I slept with a light on for the rest of that evening. The next day I mentioned this to my co-worker, wondering if there were any stories of the hotel being haunted with its long history, etc. My co-worker told me she had a strange occurrence that same night. Her experience was vastly different than mine. She wasn't scared. She awoke to find some items next to her bed displaced and her wedding ring on the floor. She rearranged her items, being sure to put her wedding ring inside her reading glasses on the nightstand. In the morning, her rings were not within her glasses where she had left them but instead were sitting NEXT to her glasses. While both of our experiences were, for the most part, harmless, I agreed with her that apparently, her ghost was a woman and fond of her jewelry. I'm not sure what my experience was about, though. Neither of us had any other paranormal activity during our last two nights there.

Another witness account of the ballroom ghost may shed some light on the origins of the hotel's ghost stories. I met this older gentleman during a book signing, and his story was quite fascinating and insightful:

In the mid-'70s, I owed a small DJ business in Albuquerque. I had been contracted to do a wedding reception at the Hotel Plaza ballroom.

I arrived about two hours before the reception was to begin to set up my sound system. The place was busy; various people were setting things up and decorating, making it a bit more difficult to get all of my stuff in place, but with a little effort, I managed to get everything ready and perform a soundcheck.

After I had finished, one of the hotel employees asked if they could unplug my gear because they needed the power outlet for a few minutes. I told them that it was not a problem as long as they didn't mess with anything. Not that I'm paranoid, but my system costs a lot of money, and I'm just a little protective of it.

I left the room and went outside to have a cigarette and chat with a buddy of mine, Eddie, who I had hired to help me out for the night. This job was one of the biggest that I had at that time, and I wanted everything to go smoothly. We discussed the song list and other details before heading back up to the ballroom. As I waited for the elevator, Eddie bolted off to the restroom, saying that he would be up in a few minutes.

Finally, the elevator door opened, and I went back upstairs. The second the door opened, I heard music coming from the ballroom. I assumed that someone had brought a boom box up there and was listening to music while they worked because the music was country. The song was a female voice singing about sunshine and birds, and I didn't have anything like that in the collection I brought to the hotel. However, when I entered the ballroom, I could not believe my eyes.

There was this redheaded chick playing the guitar on the stage, and the music was coming out of my sound system. She was dressed in a country outfit, the kind that you would see western musicians wear onstage. I immediately became angry. Somehow this woman had managed to tap into my system without my permission. There was no telling what she could have screwed up, and more than likely, I would have to do another soundcheck to correct whatever she had done.

I stormed across the ballroom, yelling at her to get off the microphone but to no avail. Either she was unable to hear me, or she didn't care. No problem, though, I thought, as I walked over to the electrical outlet to unplug the system.

When I reached the power outlet, I was shocked. The system wasn't plugged in. My hands are shaking, and suddenly, I'm afraid to look back over my shoulder at the woman. I'm pretty freaked out, this is not the kind of thing I usually would believe would happen, and I think to myself that maybe I'm just really tired, and all the caffeine is making my head do strange things. Then the music turned to static. I summoned the courage to turn around, only to discover that the woman was gone. The static noise suddenly ceased, which startled me a little, as Eddie came walking into the room. I asked him if he had seen a redhead with a guitar in the hallway, but he said that he didn't. He did hear the music and was wondering what kind of gig I had committed to.

He asked why, and I told him what happened, and his eyes get bigger and bigger. When I had finished, he told me about this old ghost story that's supposed to be this singer who died. She had played here in this very ballroom before her death.

Then he said she wrote that song we heard; it was her only hit, called "Mornin' Kind of Feelin'." Now that was pretty spooky, and just hearing that, I got the chills again. Well, anyway, that was a long time ago, but I still think of it sometimes. For a long time, I wouldn't tell anyone, my friends or the people I work with, because they'd laugh in my face and never let me hear the end of it.

This story is the oldest I have come across while researching the various ghost stories about the hotel. Because of this witness's account, I was able to track down the original ghost story. In fact, this particular ghost really got around before it wound up in the Hotel Andaluz.

The story is about Sandee Saunders, who was born on March 19, 1940, in the tiny town of Hatch, New Mexico. Her first album, *Reflections* was released in June 1972. The hit single of the album, "Mornin' Kind of Feelin'," shot up both the country and pop charts.

Before recording her album, Sandee sang at many small venues throughout New Mexico, such as the Hat Creek Saloon in Deming, the Branding Iron in Tucumcari and the Fireside Lounge in Grants. Her musical act gained popularity, and soon, Sandee was backed by her own band. They played classier tourist venues like the Hotel Plaza in Albuquerque, La Fonda in Santa Fe and the Adobe Bar at the Taos Inn.

The entry to the original ballroom. *Photo by author.*

In the early morning of August 1, 1972, tragedy struck as she drove back to Hatch after a performance in Santa Fe when her car veered off a bridge south of Caballo Lake State Park. The vehicle plunged into the Rio Grande, decapitating Sandee and flinging her body onto the opposite riverbank. Her head was never found. It is uncertain what prompted the crash, but authorities speculated that Sandee had simply fallen asleep.

Pete Pickford, Sandee's manager, was the first person to see her ghost. One morning just before dawn, he claims that he saw Sandee standing by the side of the road, signaling to him to slow down. He stepped on the brakes and looked into the rearview mirror, but the apparition was gone. Another night, he swears, Sandee's song "Mornin' Kind of Feelin'" came on the car radio just as his tires touched the bridge where she died.

Over the next several years, Sandee's ghost had an increasingly active existence. Special significance has been placed on her detached head, reportedly seen in dozens of rearview mirrors along the entire length of I-25. Her ghost has also been seen in some of the places where she had performed, including the Hotel Plaza. There, her apparition had been seen in the ballroom, wearing her pink western shirt with white fringes running under the arms. The ghost was also reported to be seen on the seventh floor, the place where she stayed after several of her performances. It bore a special significance for her, as she believed that seven was her lucky number.

Sandee is alternately regarded as a harbinger of disaster or a benevolent force given to frightening sleepy drivers awake and saving them from her sad fate.

The young musician met her fate between 2:00 and 4:00 a.m. on the bridge where Interstate 25 crosses the Rio Grande, approximately 4.3 miles northeast of Arrey, New Mexico. But her head was regularly spotted along the entire I-25 corridor throughout New Mexico, from the Texas border to Raton. In addition, psychically inclined souls have reported Sandee visitations from as far as Helsinki in Sweden to Tallahassee, Florida.

These ghostly encounters profoundly affected Pickford. He purchased Henry Saunders's old service station in Hatch. He established a small Sandee memorabilia museum, including some of her favorite stage outfits and her guitar and even placed pieces of the actual death car on display outside.

The Sandee ghost story eventually became so popular that it was featured on the TV show *Psychic Mysteries*. Additionally, the Institute for Paranormal Observation's monthly newsletter, *Glimpses*, devoted its entire August 2002 issue to Sandee-related phenomena.

The hallway of the seventh floor. Is it really a hot spot for paranormal activity? *Photo by author.*

Pete Pickford remained in Hatch until his own death in 1997, sharing stories of Sandee manifestations with everyone who stopped by the museum. However, after his death, the museum was closed. Thus the ghost stories of Sandee Saunders dwindled and were eventually forgotten.

In the Hotel Andaluz, this occurs because of the extended periods that the hotel was closed over the years for renovations as it changed owners. New staff was hired, some of whom recalled pieces of the preexisting ghost story, but this left blanks in the tale. These were eventually filled in by the staff, changing the ghost story's details slightly before the building changed hands again, repeating the process. By the time the hotel became the Andaluz, it had morphed into three different ghosts: a young woman in the ballroom, a lady in an old party dress on the seventh floor and a woman in a pink nightgown on the fourth floor.

One of the clues that led me to believe that the current stories are remnants of an older tale is the lack of details in the descriptions of the current three ghosts. The apparitions' identities are unknown in all of the accounts, with only a few details mentioned earlier in this chapter. If people saw these specters, then there should be more details in their appearance and mannerisms. Of course, they could be more allusive than the original tale. If so, the personal paranormal experiences have overwritten the original tale.

5
The Albuquerque Press Club

Tucked away on a small hill behind one of the city's mental hospitals is a unique structure that is Albuquerque's own "house on the haunted hill," the Whittlesey House, now the home of the Albuquerque Press Club.

The Whittlesey House was designed by architect Charles Whittlesey and built on his family's property in 1903 on the western edge of Albuquerque's Highlands. It is a three-story frame structure that was designed after a Norwegian villa. Low pitch roofs with exposed log fronting, rough log-cut façades and a wide porch surrounding its eastern rooms characterize the house.

For many years, the house stood virtually alone on the Highland hill, Albuquerque not having grown in that direction. There was no vegetation or trees near the house, so the view east to the Sandias and west to the town and river was unobstructed.

The *Albuquerque Morning Journal* described the house in an article titled "Bungalow Barracks" on March 24, 1903. It reads:

> *Up on the very first of the foothills that start the rise to the mesa and with a view that is unsurpassed in the Rio Grande valley, Bungalow Barracks is rapidly becoming one of the most autocratic bits of architecture in New Mexico. Charles F. Whittlesey, who owns the place, and for whose clerk and draughtsmen it is being built, is here just now to give his personal supervision to the structure, and it soon will be ready for the architects to*

The Albuquerque Press Club. *Photo by author.*

take possession. The barracks is even more attractive than the plans would have indicated. There are no smooth boards in the place. It is all rough pine logs with the bark on, and it is built with the fewest number of nails possible. Whenever it is possible, the logs are put together with wooden bolts, and there are all the picturesque features of the old-time log cabin with a whole lot of modern conveniences. For instance, the fireplace in the living room, made in the roughest possible style of the unhewn black rock from the lava bed over east, is reinforced by a very modern and well-built steam heating plant so that one may have the picturesque without any of the usual discomforts of a frosted back. This living room is a marvel of light in spite of the low ceilings and deep windows. These windows face the four winds and command the best views of the valley that can be had. The dining room looks down over the town, and the valley and the sleeping rooms are all light and airy. Around it all is a deep veranda, built of rough logs like the rest, and the most attractive feature of the house for here is the promise of cool summer days when the valley below is roasting and of equally comfortable summer nights. It is going to be the very swellest little clubhouse in New Mexico and will be one of the sights. The barn-like house is built of rough logs, and it will give room for a dozen of the hill ponies that the architects use for their outings.

In 1908, the Whittlesey sold to Theodore S. Woolsey Jr., who owned the house for the next twelve years. Some early photos suggest that Theodore added the addition to the south side of the house and framed out the northwest corner of the main porch. Historical records also show that he leased the house to Mr. Andros, president of Whitney Hardware, in 1916.

Albuquerque was known nationwide for its good climate, which was believed to be conducive to treating certain diseases such as tuberculosis. Located on the Highland near the house was the Albuquerque Sanitarium. The head nurse at the sanitarium passed the house each day on her way to work, and she quickly fell in love with the place, so much that she informed a suitor that if he bought the "log" house, she would marry him. Arthur B. Hall bought the house from Woolsey in 1920, and she married him. Clifford Hall, A.B.'s wife, lived in and eventually owned the house during the next forty years. During those years, she brought the house through periods of extensive remodeling and changes of the interior's style.

Not all was well in Clifford's life, though, as her success in love often seemed to fall short. In 1930, Clifford was divorced from A.B. Hall. By 1935, she was remarried to Herbert McCallum, but this too would end in divorce in 1938.

As a source of income during these years, she would rent out portions of the house. The south porch was framed out and part of the first level was sealed off to make a separate apartment. The original stable was renovated and added to, making it an apartment complex, and an additional apartment was built adjacent to it.

During the following years, Clifford resurfaced the interior walls of the house. Celotex, plaster and wood planking covered the building's rough wood and burlap surfaces. By the middle of the '40s, the rough wood floors were resurfaced with oak strip flooring. Knotty pine siding was introduced to some wall surfaces. The colors of gold and red were accentuated through new furniture and draperies. Marble-topped European furniture pieces filled the main room. This, of all the rooms in the house, was visually the richest. The immense lava rock fireplace, the filled bookshelves lining the walls and the rustic hark wall surfaces were contrasted against the floor's gold and reds, furniture, draperies and incidentals.

During the '30s, '40s and '50s, the Highland Park "log" house was a showplace, and Clifford spent a great deal of time in her house and its surroundings.

In 1960, Clifford sold the house. Her increasing age, the extensive upkeep on the structure and numerous other reasons contributed to her decision.

The Zeta Mu Zeta House Corporation of the Lambda Chi Alpha Fraternity purchased the house as soon as it was put up for sale. The building's apartment-like situation suited the fraternity's interests perfectly. Eventually, though, the fraternity moved closer to the University of New Mexico. They sold the house in 1966 to John T. Roberson, who leased the structure for the next several years. The Albuquerque Press Club eventually purchased the Whittlesey House in the 1970s.

The majority of the ghostly activity at the Press Club seems to be centered near the bar area. One evening around eight o'clock, one of the bartenders, Mary, rinsed some glasses that she had just washed. The business was slow that night; there were only four patrons in the building, one of whom was Mary's husband. The three men were engaged in light conversation when Mary suddenly felt a strange, unusual sensation. The sensation was so intense that she stopped what she was doing and stared at the room directly in front of the bar. She could faintly hear the sound of footsteps, similar to those of a woman walking on a wooden floor with high heels. As she tried to focus on the sound's exact location, she saw a shadowy image of a woman in a black dress in her peripheral vision. She turned and watched the ghostly image as it walked across the adjoining room, frozen in fear. Her husband glanced up and noticed her expression and posture and asked her what was wrong.

When Mary didn't answer, he turned to look in the same direction that she was. "There she is—the ghost! Look!" he called out as the woman in black turned away, making a quick exit toward the far wall. As the other men turned around, the spectral figure vanished, leaving no trace. It was an experience that Mary never forgot.

Other bartenders at the club have seen the mysterious woman in black as well, including one of the bar managers. Christina worked as the club's bar manager for about five months when she had her first encounter with the ghost. It was around 3:00 a.m. when Christina and Kent, then the club's president, were leisurely caught up in a conversation. The building was empty, all of the patrons had long gone, and the house was locked up for the night.

As the two chatted, Christina suddenly noticed that someone was looking at them from the other end of the room. As she stood up to face the person, she saw a woman dressed in a black cape or dress. The woman in black quickly moved away, gradually vanishing as she left. The entire incident lasted only seconds. As Christina sat back down, Kent asked, "What's going on?" The only thing that Christina could think to say was, "I think I just saw

Albuquerque's own house on a haunted hill. *Photo by author.*

a ghost!" Very casually, Kent replied, "Oh, that's just Mrs. M. Just leave her a shot of gin on the bar, as I do."

After Christina had calmed down, Kent told her of his experiences with the ghost of the house. He described hearing footsteps and seeing fleeting images of the woman in black, who he believed was Clifford's ghost or Mrs. M, a nickname the patrons have given her. The only way he could think to appease the ghost was by leaving a shot of gin for her on the bar. Sometimes she drinks it; sometimes she doesn't.

So, Christina took Kent's advice and poured a single shot of gin, leaving it on the bar. At nine o'clock the following morning, Christina returned to the club to prepare some paperwork for the accountant. She was the first person in that morning, and after making some coffee, she sat down to go over the paperwork. It was then that she remembered the shot of gin. She got up and walked over to the bar, where she had placed the shot the night before. It was empty. She held it up to the light to see if there were any lip prints along the rim.

There were none. Since then, it has been a tradition for the bartender to occasionally leave the shot of gin for the house's unseen resident.

Other unusual events have centered on a pool table in the recreation room of the house. Pool balls have been heard moving about when no one was in the area.

Another common impression is the feeling of being watched in certain areas of the house. With its unique architecture, the house has several unusual "closets" that open into a bigger area than one would expect. Many of these are access areas for water and electrical lines. The club has always had a pet cat. The first was named Emma, and she would stare intently at an empty corner of the room before drawing back her ears and hissing at an unseen presence. The current cat sometimes displays similar actions, although not nearly as frequently as Emma.

From what I have been able to ascertain, the ghost story's beginnings started in the late 1980s. It was relatively unknown until its ghost stories were published in *Adobe Angels: Ghosts of Albuquerque* by Antonio Garcez. While it is a good ghost story, the original participants have long since moved on. These days, nothing is occurring that is quite as dramatic. While some people I have spoken to have felt a female presence, many others do not believe that the building is haunted.

You might have noticed the folklore influence of leaving an offering or libation for the dead, a shot of gin in this case. These acts can have a variety of purposes and are quite common in New Mexico. On the one hand, they are made to a spirit to give thanks and to show honor and respect. The idea is to build a relationship with the spirit and thus ensure their good favor for the future.

On the other hand, offerings can be an act of appeasement to a spirit in the hope that they will leave you alone. It is the concept of do ut habeas, "I give that thou mayest be gone."

According to folklore, some spirits might appreciate a token of respect and agree to peaceful terms so long as the living keep showing them respect. Or perhaps Mrs. M is just particular about the people with whom she interacts.

6
The Old Bernalillo County Courthouse

Bernalillo County was established on January 8, 1852. It was one of the seven Partidos established during the Mexican rule of the state. It was possibly named for the Gonzales-Bernal family that lived in the area before 1692. The county seat is Albuquerque.

The first courthouse in Albuquerque was built in 1886 at the cost of $62, 053.81 and was constructed of gray stone with a peaked shingled roof exterior tower reaching three stories high. The courthouse stood at the current San Felipe Elementary School site in Old Town. Once the demand for another school surfaced, the courthouse was relocated to New Town (present-day downtown area).

This "new" courthouse was built in 1926, with bricks imported from Colorado. Built in the center of its own park, the symmetrical design gave the building a Grecian temple of justice look. In 1964, the courthouse was remodeled and expanded. Its outer surface was also refinished with sheets of marble. A more modern courthouse was built and completed in 2001, leaving the older building empty.

In 2003, the community service group was assigned the task of cleaning out the old courthouse downtown and removing assorted furniture and other items left behind when the building was vacated. Dan Byers was the man who supervised the juvenile delinquents who were doing their community service work by cleaning up the building so the county could lease it out. These kids were hardcore, not just shoplifters or vandals, but criminals who have stabbed or even shot people. The groups of cleaners were not the types who would be easily frightened. However, in the basement rooms, they collectively witnessed strange things.

As Byers and his crew cleared out a room, the doors were closed and locked. Except for the maintenance crew, no one else had access to the building, yet it was not unusual for them to return the next day and discover that doors were reopened and lights turned back on.

One afternoon, a female delinquent had been sent to clean out a set of large file cabinets in one of the offices on the basement floor. She returned shortly after, saying that the cabinets had moved by themselves and that she would not go back into that room. She appeared to be quite shaken up and very serious about not returning to the office.

Another unusual event occurred one afternoon while Byers and a colleague rounded up the kids to do a headcount before taking lunch. All of the kids were present and accounted for when suddenly something slammed onto the floor with a loud bang. Byers turned to see an old law book sliding into the entry of the doorway. It spun around a few times before finally coming to a halt. Byers immediately stuck his head out the door; however, the hallway was empty. The law book was from the 1920s, and the area where it stopped became a cold zone. For days, no one was willing to touch it.

The old Bernalillo County Courthouse. *Wikimedia Commons.*

The basement hallway seems to be a significant focus of the haunting. At the western end of the hall, an apparition of a little girl has been spotted several times by different people. She is described as an adorable girl, perhaps six or seven years old, with blond hair in pigtails. She wears a white blouse that resembles a school uniform and has an aura of sadness that radiates from her. Oddly enough, that area of the old courthouse once housed the divorce court.

Other strange occurrences have been experienced by various people who have dared to venture into the dark recesses of the basement. One woman was feeling for a light switch along a wall when she felt someone take her hand and place it on the switch. When she turned on the light, no one was there. Another room suddenly began emitting a horrendous odor for no apparent reason and became so cold that visitors could see their breath. Objects continued to be moved, and areas that had been cleaned up had been tampered with. Eventually, Byers became concerned that this might be the work of a transient, so he checked the building for broken or open windows. After a thorough search of the building, he found no signs that someone was living there, no evidence of food, liquor, clothing or bedding. The building was entirely secure.

Two people reportedly died in the building, both of heart attacks. One was a former sheriff who passed on at his desk in the basement, and the other is an unidentified man who met his death on one of the upper floors.

The cleanup workers tried doing little "tests" by placing objects in certain places, placing a dry eraser on a doorknob, etc., and then returning to find these objects moved. Other things that have been experienced are cold spots, hot spots, lights being turned off, doors being closed and locked when a key is required and boxes that were taped closed being opened and contents strewn about.

After the courthouse was renovated, sections of the building were opened and rented out as business offices. The hauntings, particularly that of the little girl ghost, still occur in the building's historic halls. One of the workers there, who asked not to be identified, told me this story about her experience with the spirit of the little girl:

> *I am thirty-two years old and have had several occurrences in my life, which I can't explain and have bothered me. I was working in an office in the old courthouse when unusual things began occurring. Often my job had me working well into the evening, and during the winter months, it was frequently dark before I went home.*

One evening I was working late and had called my boyfriend to ask him if he could pick up some fast food and bring it over. I had a lot of filing that had to be done by the next morning, and this way, I could make the most of my time and hopefully be finished before 10:00.

About thirty minutes later, he called me, informing me that he was outside. The doors are kept locked in the evening, so I had to go downstairs and let him in.

I escorted him back up to my office so we could eat together, but as we turned the corner to the hallway leading to the office, I was suddenly horrified. There were papers and files strewn all over the hallway. I ran back to the office and confirmed my worst fear. The mess in the hall was indeed the stack of papers that I had in my inbox to file. At first, I thought that there might have been an open window and a sudden gust of air may have blown the papers from my desk. We checked the windows, and all of them were closed. The doors to the other offices were closed and locked so that no breezes could have come from them. The oddest thing was that I could smell ozone in the room, overpowering the scent of age and mildew.

At that time, I didn't think that it was a ghost. It was just an unusual occurrence. Then, several weeks later, I had a more profound experience.

I was leaving late again, as usual, and as I came down the final flight of stairs, I noticed the sound of a small child crying. This was strange because, to the best of my knowledge, I was alone in the building.

Fearing that someone had left their child in an office, I listened and tried to follow the sound to its source. It was coming up the stairwell from the basement. It only took me a moment to get to the basement, but most of the lights were off. The crying suddenly stopped before I was able to determine which direction the sound was coming from. I strained my eyes to look for the child as I called out, asking if anyone was there. I started down the west corridor when I suddenly had a strange feeling that someone was standing by me. I turned around to see a small blond-headed girl, maybe seven years old or so, standing there staring at me. The girl's face was mouthing words, words I could not hear but instead feel. She was calling for her mother in a soul-wrenching, desperate voice that was emoted to me, at once searing my soul and sending icy shards stabbing up my spine. Horribly, she reminded me of my daughter, in the custody of her father after a long and bitter divorce.

As I started to move toward her, she simply vanished into thin air. That was when I realized that I had just seen a ghost. As strange as it may sound, I wasn't frightened or anything. There was just this profuse feeling of sadness.

In time, she began making her appearances outside the windows when I was working late at night. It did not matter if I closed the blinds, the mysterious iridescent figure appeared, and I could hear the sounds of her weeping, ripping out my heart and freezing my soul with her palpable sadness and longing.

Several times I tried to communicate with her, but she seemed to be unable to. These ghostly visits were not frequent, but when they happened, it affected me for days afterward.

I finally quit my job because I couldn't handle the emotional landslide and depression that would result from the brief encounters with the ghost.

The old courthouse was a functional building for the county until 2001, when the new courthouse was built nearby. Since then, it's been the backdrop in popular movies and TV shows like *Better Call Saul* and is one of the stops on the downtown ghost tour. At one point, it even served as a haunted house attraction for Halloween.

In August 2020, the building was sold for $647,500. However, the county negotiated a contract with the new owners to lease the building for various film productions for the next year. It will be interesting to see if the ghost stories continue as the old building evolves for another purpose.

7
Mount Calvary Cemetery

In 1869, the Jesuit fathers in Albuquerque declared that they would be building a new chapel and cemetery. The old cemetery, located near the San Felipe de Neri Church, was full and would no longer accept new burials. So, the search for a new cemetery began. Soon, Father Donato Gasparri located a suitable site three miles to the east of the Old Townsite. The majority of the bodies from the old grounds were carefully moved in 1869. It was quite a task, as almost two tons of remains were exhumed from a cemetery near Old Town to be reburied here when the original resting place was sold off. The original and oldest section is called Santa Barbara Cemetery.

The first recorded interment was in August 1870. The earliest existing monuments are those of Vicente Otero (1877), Jesusita Baca de Romero (1877) and Diego Armijo (1878).

In 1936, the Reverend Libertini chaired a committee to modernize and beautify the cemetery. In 1938, a solemn high Mass dedicated the new chapel and cemetery. The parishes of San Felipe and the Immaculate Conception used Santa Barbara Cemetery, which later became a part of the newer, larger Mount Calvary Cemetery.

The new cemetery consisted of an additional eighteen acres of land north of the older Santa Barbara portion. A new chapel was built in 1992 as well as a mausoleum. The original business office is now a columbarium for cremated remains.

The oldest section of Mount Calvary Cemetery is known as the Santa Barbara Cemetery. *Photo by author.*

Mount Calvary is a nonsectarian perpetual care cemetery. Various priests in the city celebrate a monthly Mass on the first Saturday of each month. The cemetery is dedicated to fostering communication, cooperation and service, as well as being responsive to the changing needs of the people.

The oldest section of the graveyard is where an unusual specter has chosen to haunt the living. It is a shadowy apparition of a man who wears a hat and suit. Stranger still, the ghost holds a tattered rope in its hands, which leads to a noose that is firmly attached to its neck. According to witnesses, the spirit is seen moving about the old section of the cemetery late at night when the moon is full.

A young woman named Marina, a student at the University of New Mexico, witnessed one late-night encounter:

> *My husband and I were driving around on Edith Street one evening as I needed to complete my Night Photography assignment for a class that I was taking. I had taken a few pictures downtown and decided to take some night shots of the cemetery down the road. It was only 10:40 p.m., very early by my standards. We turned into the cemetery driveway, but the gates were closed. I was more inclined to turn back, but my husband insisted on staying. He got out of the car first while I was fumbling with my camera.*
>
> *Before I could get out of the car, my husband immediately got back in and yelled at me to stay put. I could sense something was definitely wrong.*

His face was white, and his voice was very shaky as he fumbled with the car keys as he put them into the ignition. I started getting goosebumps when something happened. I got some kind of an alert, a sixth sense registered something, and I turned and looked to my right. As I looked out of the passenger side window, I saw a faint figure walking toward us, coming out of the cemetery. He was wearing a hat and a suit, his skin was grayish, and his face seemed to have an expression of being in pain. In his hands, I could clearly see a rope that was tied onto his neck. It only lasted for a couple of seconds, but I got a distinct feeling that I had just seen a ghost.

We immediately drove out of the area, and while doing so, my husband asked me if I had noticed a strong smell of burnt hair. I shook my head and asked him what was going on. He said he saw the same figure that I had seen, except he noticed that the figure was walking through tombstones as it approached. We both drove back to our house in silence, and I feared that the thing might follow us home.

Although the spirit is unidentified, there might be a clue tucked away in the city's ancient past.

New Albuquerque started as a depot, built in 1880 by the Atchison, Topeka and Santa Fe Railway. Soon afterward, frame buildings such as the L.B. Putney warehouse, Girard's Restaurant and the Maden House hotel were erected nearby. Suddenly, what had been a train stop was a town with businesses, prospects and crime.

In the spring of 1818, Lieutenant John G. Bourke got off the train in Albuquerque just in time to see "two high-toned gentlemen of the town blazing away at each other" up the street. "Unfortunately," Bourke later wrote, "neither was killed."

The leading citizens of New Albuquerque quickly decided that they needed a town marshal to keep law and order, to protect decent folks from the deliberate or errant shots of the drifting riffraff who floated through western boomtowns at that time. They chose Milt Yarberry, a man in his early thirties, because he was available and knew which side of a six-gun to point at the bad guys. Not much else seemed to qualify him.

Very little is known of Yarberry's life before he became Albuquerque's first marshal, but what is known is shady at best. Several nasty rumors circulated concerning several rustlings and shooting scrapes on the Texas-Arkansas border in his youth. Between 1876 and 1881, he ran a saloon and billiards hall in Texas and, afterward, a dance hall in the town of Bernalillo, New Mexico.

What is known is that shortly after he arrived in New Albuquerque, he became the town's marshal and was indicted for murder shortly after that. It started on March 27, 1881, when Yarberry gunned down a loudmouthed, well-connected young man named Harry Brown near Girard's Restaurant at Second Street and Railroad Avenue (now called Central Street).

Brown's crime was that he was Yarberry's rival for Sadie Preston's affections. She was a beautiful widow residing in the area, and Milt was quite jealous and possessive. Brown, who worked on trains as a messenger for an express company, had been quite egotistical since foiling a train robbery in Kansas in 1878. Witnesses say it was Brown who initiated the faceoff with Yarberry on that Sunday evening in March.

"I want you to understand I am not afraid of you and would not be even if you were marshal of the United States," one witness reported hearing Brown say to Yarberry. Some accounts say a witness heard Brown slap Yarberry.

Everybody in the vicinity heard the shots, four of them, all fired by Yarberry, two or three of them after Brown was on the ground. Unfortunately for Yarberry, Brown was a well-connected man. He was the son of Neil S. Brown, a former governor of Tennessee who had also served as U.S. minister to Russia, and the nephew of John C. Brown, a prominent man in the railroad business. Fortunately, in the murder trial that followed, Yarberry

The graves of the original town site were relocated here in late 1869. Photo by author.

was acquitted after witnesses testified that Brown had promised to kill Yarberry on sight.

Still, it galled the respectable citizens of New Albuquerque that Yarberry could get away with killing someone from such an influential family. What would the rest of the country think of a town that lets something like that happen? After the trial, Yarberry resumed his duties as town marshal, but there were plenty of people just waiting to pounce on him the next time he made a slip. They didn't have to wait long.

Less than three months after he killed Brown, Yarberry shot down Charles D. Campbell, a railroad carpenter, at Railroad Avenue and First Street. He had been shot three times, twice in the back. Witnesses said that after shooting Campbell, Yarberry danced around and yelled, "I've downed the son of a bitch."

The incident started when Yarberry and a gambler named Frank Boyd went to investigate a shot that had been fired in or near the Greenleaf Restaurant on First Street, just south of Railroad Avenue. As they approached the scene, someone pointed out Campbell, who was crossing First Street, as the man they wanted.

Yarberry claims that he got within ten steps of the man and ordered him to hold up his hands. The man then turned and said, "You hold up your hands." Yarberry's suspect then drew a gun and fired five or six shots. Yarberry returned fire, shooting Campbell five times. He then shot Campbell two or three more times after he was down.

The controversy started immediately after Campbell's pistol could not be found, and no one ever knew for sure if he had fired the shot that started the whole business. Most witnesses to the event claimed that Yarberry went at Campbell from behind, ordered him to put up his hands and started shooting.

Yarberry was arrested but did not go to trial for this killing until May 1882. The trial lasted three days, and after deliberating for only an hour, the jury came back with a guilty verdict. District judge Joseph Bell sentenced Yarberry to be hanged.

Yarberry's lawyer appealed the verdict while his client was held in the Santa Fe Jail while the legal matters ran their course.

He escaped on September 9, 1882, but was recaptured a few days later at Arroyo Galisteo. On February 9, 1883, a train to Albuquerque returned him for his execution, set for that day at the Bernalillo County Jail, just east of the Plaza in Old Town.

At about 2:40 p.m., he was taken to the jail's courtyard, which had been boarded off from public view for the occasion. One hundred people had obtained tickets to view the hanging but hundreds more watched from nearby rooftops and trees.

The gallows, a new design based on plans that had appeared in an issue of *Scientific American*, was different than the standard gallows of the time. The hanging victim on this "improved gallows" was yanked upward when a 325-pound weight was dropped, instead of plunging to his death through a trapdoor in the floor.

Once the noose was on his neck, Yarberry was asked if he had any last words. Yarberry talked for fifteen minutes. "Friends, you are about to hang Milt Yarberry," he said. "You are not going to hang him for the murder of Campbell but for the killing of Brown."

He was still talking when they put the black hood over his head. "Gentlemen, you are hanging an innocent man," was the last thing Yarberry said through the black cloth before he was executed.

However, the execution did not go as planned. The 325-pound weight severed Milt's head from his body. The black hood, with Milt's head still inside, went flying off the gallows and into the expectant crowd. The rope itself cinched so tightly around the vertebrae of his neck that no one was able to remove it. The spectacle astonished and horrified the crowd of participants. It was to be the last public execution in Albuquerque.

In the end, Milt Yarberry, the first town marshal of New Albuquerque, was buried in the Santa Barbara Cemetery with the hanging rope still clenched around his neck.

The history makes sense because, in some instances, the ghost is seen missing its head. As one approaches the cemetery, it used to be hard not to notice broken sections of the cemetery's low wall. Some of these might be attributed to driving under the influence, but Milt's ghost is rumored to be responsible for several as well.

A story told by a woman named Christy is a typical example:

> *I haven't really had many personal experiences with the paranormal, which is a shame really, because I've always been fascinated by the subject. Ever since I was a kid, I've loved scary movies and loved the adrenaline rush that comes from being scared. However, the thought of being haunted by a poltergeist or waking to a ghostly figure sitting at the foot of my bed isn't really appealing either, so I guess I'm good with the experience I had.*

Haunted Albuquerque

It happened while I was attending the University of New Mexico in 1985. After class one day, I overheard a conversation that involved the word "ghost." My ears perked up, and I requested a quick summation of what happened. I got the location of the ghostly sighting and the steps one must take to see the ghost. The ghost appears at a residential intersection, Odelia Road and Edith, but you must follow specific driving instructions in order to see it. The instructions were as follows: Drive on Odelia going west, past Edith Street until you get to Broadway Boulevard. Then, you make a U-turn back toward Edith, but you must turn off your headlights while doing so. Then, slowly creep back to Edith and turn left, and a ghostly headless figure will appear on that corner, leaning up against the cemetery wall.

So, that evening, despite the rain, I gathered two friends, who I'll call Brian and Will, and off we went. All of us were reasonably skeptical and didn't expect to see anything. We followed the instructions and started our slow creep back to Edith. When we arrived at the street, we turned left. It's a quiet neighborhood, so we sat there for a minute, then we started to see a silhouette appear, then it took on a little more definition. At this point, my friends and I start freaking out, panicked and took off. That is when things took a turn for the worse. As Brian hit the accelerator, he lost control of the car on the wet road. The car jumped the curb and crashed into the cemetery wall, just past the place where the headless figure stood. I heard Will scream, "He is coming toward us," as Brian frantically put the car in reverse. He quickly got us back onto the road, and we left the area at a high rate of speed.

After a few minutes and a few miles down the road, we gathered our composure and decided to try again, thinking our minds must have been playing tricks on us. We thought maybe our outbursts and comments during the initial sighting fed each other's imagination.

We followed the directions again and sat silently in my car after we made the turn onto Edith, staring at the cemetery wall. Then it starts to happen again. Almost as clear as day, a man's body with no head appears, leaning against the wall. We could clearly see what appeared to be a rope hanging from what remained of his neck. His arms were down by his side, then, all of a sudden, he crossed them. At the same time, all three of us said, "Oh crap, did you just see that!" Yea, we all saw it. Arms crossed, that did it for us. I have never gone back since.

Milt Yarberry's unmarked grave is rumored to be near the southeast corner of the graveyard. *Photo by author.*

Other sightings of the ghost have placed him standing in the middle of the road. Supposedly, drivers have had to veer off to avoid hitting, and a few are rumored to have hit the short wall that used to surround the graveyard. A decorative metal fence has now replaced the wall.

Many believe that Milt Yarberry haunts the area because he swore a curse on everyone who took part in the trial. According to the legend, everyone who was involved in that trial met a violent or untimely death. His angry spirit still roams the old part of the cemetery seeking retribution for his "unjustified" execution. Others claim that he is searching for his tombstone, which was mysteriously removed from the graveyard many decades ago. It is still missing today, and the exact location of Yarberry's grave is not known. This is interesting, as the folklore of some cultures believe placing a tombstone on the grave keeps the ghost weighed down.

The cemetery also has quite a few curiosities. One unusual crypt has an active phone line running into it. The deceased had provisions put into his will that paid for the installation of the line and for five years of service. That way, if he "woke up" and was not actually dead, he could call his relatives to come and get him out.

A new section dedicated to the Lady of Guadalupe will have a selection of indoor mausoleum crypts, outdoor crypts, outdoor niches, family estates and ground burial spaces for caskets and cremated remains. The building has a beautiful stained-glass window depicting the Lady of Guadalupe and St. Juan Diego's image. The granite façades have been imported from Italy.

While there are many alternative explanations for the ghostly activity that people have reported here, it is a unique part of Albuquerque's history and worth visiting. It contains gravesites of famous New Mexicans, such as Dennis Chavez, Solomon Luna and Randy Castillo, the drummer for Ozzy Osbourne for nearly a decade.

8
Old Albuquerque High School

As New Albuquerque flourished, the railroad assigned Colonel Marmon to lay out some city streets. He laid one street parallel to the horse car line, which he called Central, and the first road west of the tracks and running parallel he named First Street. Although the railroad did not request any roads east of the tracks, this is where Marmon plotted his widest street.

He named that street Broadway and proceeded to develop four streets east of it. He named the first street Arno after Arno Huning, who was a pioneer businessman in Albuquerque. The next two streets he named after his children, Edith and Walter, and his last street was named High.

By 1881, the population of Albuquerque was one thousand. At that time, there were few high schools, primarily because it was difficult to obtain funds. The result was that the existing schools were privately funded. The first organized school was started in 1879 on the east side of the plaza in a donated section of the Ambrosio Armijo Store and house by the Colorado College of Colorado Springs. Thus were the beginnings of what was to become Albuquerque High. Twenty-seven students enrolled.

In 1881, the academy moved out of Old Town to New Town to accommodate the shifting of families who were flocking to the businesses and housing generated by the railroad. This school conducted classes into an adobe building on Lead between Third and Fourth for just over a year before it was moved again to a larger structure on Silver Street between Fifth and Sixth Streets.

Old Albuquerque High School in 2017. *Creative Commons.*

The academy was operated by a seventeen-member board of trustees composed of business and professional men whose chief purpose seemed to be to give the town as good a school as possible. The academy was a tuition school, but the tuition never supported it adequately, and the difference had to be made up from the pockets of the trustees, friends or the resource of the New West Association, which supported the Colorado College. The academy had a primary, intermediate and a college preparatory department. The college preparatory division charged a tuition of three dollars per month for the ordinary course and an additional one dollar per month if the student took the special French and German course. If the student wished, he could take twenty-four music lessons during the year for an additional fee of eighteen dollars. (In 1860, one dollar per day was considered to be a fair wage.)

In 1886, the academy's curriculum listed such subjects as English, history, algebra, geometry, bookkeeping, physiology, rhetoric, botany, physics, political science, civil government, American and English literature, French, German, Latin and Greek. School activities were chiefly provided by sedate music recitals and equally sedate debating contests. Boys were encouraged in playground sports such as baseball, but there were no competitive teams.

In 1890, the academy moved into a new building at Central and Edith, where the public library is now located. It operated there for just over a year before the city received the power to levy taxes for school funds. The city then took over the whole operation, and Professor Hodgen was appointed the new city superintendent of schools. While the academy had been privately owned, it had been operated by local authorities and primarily supported locally for the interests of the community.

By 1891, the population of Albuquerque had grown to four thousand. The town had twenty saloons and two banks, one of which went broke during the panic of 1893. The University of New Mexico was started, and the high school and the university had developed a good relationship of cooperation.

The new Albuquerque High was housed on the third floor of the old city library building, and in 1892, the first graduating class consisted of three members: Mabel Daniels, Lu Hughes and Mildred Whiteman.

In 1893, the school was moved to a frame building in the 200 block of South Edith, where it remained for six or seven years. In the fall of 1900, it was moved to the central school building at Third and Lead, where it was located until 1914. This building later became an office for the superintendent of schools.

By 1895, Albuquerque had twenty-three saloons and had almost as many gambling establishments. People were moving to Albuquerque for health reasons, and the city was taking on many aspects of larger eastern cities. Even after the 1900s, there were still occasional stage holdups, and by 1903, there had been two cases of school money embezzling by the city's officials. One hundred dollars was spent on advertising the Albuquerque schools at the World's Fair in 1893, and in 1908, the city's educational exhibits won first prize in the International Industrial Exposition.

In 1914, Old Main was built. Along the north side of the building, about where Copper Street is, ran an arroyo. On the north side of the arroyo was Pence Wagon Yard, which was used to house the mules and otherwise provide for their needs. The south side of the arroyo is where the gym steps are now and where Old Main was built.

The school was heavily criticized for building a facility that was too large. The campus comprised five buildings grouped around a central courtyard at the intersection of Central and Broadway. One thing was for certain— the school building was going to satisfy the educational needs of the town for quite a time. Just east of Pence Wagon Yard were some weather-beaten houses (current location of the gym), and it was rumored that a treasure was buried there. Over the years, this area has been the scene of intensive search efforts in man's never-ending quest for quick wealth. The arroyo, which ran along the north side, was quite deep, and it often was the ground used for settling disputes. In 1915, it was the meeting place of two rival gangs, the Capulets and the Montagues, and in 1917, the rival gangs who used the area were the Hatfields and the McCoys.

In 1914, the town's population was ten thousand, and grades nine through twelve were being educated in the building on Central Avenue. However, by 1917, the county population had increased by two thousand, and paving became a sign of the times. Central Avenue was paved from Eighth Street to approximately where the Presbyterian Hospital is currently located, and Fourth Street was paved from Mountain to Coal. However, the majority of the town streets remained unpaved.

John Milne became superintendent early in his career in Albuquerque. Appointed in 1911, he remained in that post well over forty years.

The first edition of the *La Reata* was printed in 1909 by a local establishment and was financed mostly by advertising. In 1917, the school began instruction in printing, and in 1918, the first *La Reata* was printed by the instructors and students at Albuquerque High School. The school printed it until 1959. The first newspaper produced by Albuquerque High came out in 1902 and was published until 1907. The title of this early newspaper was the *Occident*, and no copies of this remain. During the school year 1919–20, Miss Oliver Morris started the *Record*, which remains the official and only school newspaper. The first issue was published on September 28, 1919.

The armistice ending World War I was signed in 1918, and everyone was dealing with the postwar activities, which were universal. The manual arts classes during the year 1918–19 constructed four dozen tables for the Red Cross to be used for wounded soldiers. Despite the tragedy of the war, the populace was still trying to put sunshine in its life, and the era of jazz was already afoot. The school was part of this movement. It had its version of a jazz band called the Ukelele Orchestra.

The class of 1920 included students who represented thirty-six states and ten countries. The Roosevelt and Webster debating societies were organized in 1919, and most people in the school belonged to one or the other. Both of these societies continued until 1940.

The school was relocated in the 1970s, leaving the old campus empty. It was not treated well; most of the windows were broken out by vandals and bored teenagers, and the buildings became something of an eyesore.

After sitting empty for three decades, the school has now been converted to an ambitious loft apartment complex, marking a victory for preservationists who feared the landmark buildings would be demolished. Alumni were offered the first choice of the newly renovated lofts. The lofts used the classroom space as apartments while the interior spaces, such as the main library room and gymnasium spaces, were preserved as landmarks.

Several locations that were occupied by the school over the years also have reputations of being haunted. The first is located in a shop in Old Town, where the school occupied Armijo store and house. The shop is called La Piñata. It features custom eighteenth-century Native American porcelain dolls, Indian jewelry, leather goods, piñatas, flowers and paintings among its wares. However, the building is believed to be haunted by several spirits.

One evening, the new owner of the business was sorting her inventory in the back storeroom when the ladder she was standing on was forcibly pushed out from underneath her. She managed to escape injury but felt an unseen evil presence afterward, mostly when she was alone in the store. Distraught, she called a friend who helped her locate a local Native medicine man who eventually removed the evil spirit from the building.

However, the Native ritual did not remove all of the spirits from the historic building. One, in particular, made his presence known in more ways than one. The shop owner believes that this spirit is the ghost of a little boy who frequented this place during his lifetime. The ghost is harmless, and at his worst, he is nothing more than a nuisance.

His favorite activity seems to be playing with the many dolls and piñatas in the store. Often, the shop owner would arrive early in the morning to open up for the day's business, only to discover that many of the dolls were in disarray. Several of them were heaped in a pile in the center of the floor, while others were placed in odd locations.

Once again, the owner consulted the medicine man, who recommended that the spirit be left an offering to keep it docile. So, the owner began leaving a small dish filled with candy on the counter near the register at night. When she returned in the morning, the dolls were in the exact places where she had left them the night before, but the candy dish was empty.

Another haunted location is Old Main itself. When the structure was still a dilapidated building, I had a former student, now in his sixties, tell me this story:

> When I attended the old High School, there were lots of rumors of the buildings being haunted, especially Old Main. During my freshman year, I didn't experience any paranormal activity, but there was this eerie feeling that someone is watching me. This was especially true even when you are

all alone in the boys' restroom, which is creepy enough by itself. At times I caught myself glancing over my shoulder to see who was behind me while using the urinal. For no apparent reason, I would get goosebumps and could feel my hair standing on end. Although it's unsettling and a little spooky, I didn't feel threatened or in danger. Most of my other classmates would say the same thing, but we would just shrug it off. It was probably just the ambiance of the building.

During my sophomore year, I was walking through the Main's deserted corridors after classes with a friend, looking for a particular teacher. All the classrooms we passed were closed for the day and locked. Then, as we passed by a locked office near the end of the hall, we both clearly heard someone furiously tapping away on a typewriter inside. We were curious because we saw that the lights inside were off. What made this so strange is that there is a locked padlock outside that door. So how could anyone be inside a dark room typing on a typewriter? We looked at each other and ran out of that building as fast as we can.

Not long after hearing this story, the Southwest Ghost Hunter's Association was contacted by a foreman involved with the renovation of Old Main and the other buildings on campus. He claimed that he was having trouble keeping employees because of unusual occurrences that scared them off the job. The occurrences included darting shadows, disembodied footsteps and tools that would go missing, only to be found in sections where the employees were not working.

Although the ghost hunters could not find anything paranormal, the stories of ghosts and paranormal activity have continued.

Several other legends have arisen about the "hauntings" of the old high school. One such tale involves a teacher who fell in love with a student and then hanged himself. His ghost supposedly still haunts Old Main. Another story involves a girl who was mixed up in a love triangle with a married teacher. Yet another tells of a boy who died by suicide in the gym. No one seems to be sure just how the stories got started, but they seem to have spread after the school was relocated and the old buildings stood empty.

I was on the team that investigated some of the structures that were reported to be haunted. While we did not find anything that would indicate that the buildings were haunted, I can see how easy it would be for someone to get spooked in them. The wind whistles about in odd patterns as it enters a broken window, moves through the halls and eventually out another window. The interior halls were dark with a bright light beaming through in intervals. At one point, I thought I saw an "odd shadow" but determined that it was an illusion created by lighting contrasts in the building while I was walking through the halls.

I was also able to walk through some of the apartments after they were completed. The apartments are quite beautiful and have none of the creepy ambiance that I experienced on my previous visit.

9
FAIRVIEW CEMETERY

Graveyards and cemeteries are among some of the most haunted places, according to folklore and superstition. However, the desecrated graveyard appears to be even more so. The Duke City has more than its share of haunted burial sites, and in these come a variety of ghostly tales. When supported by a macabre or obscure fact, they can become even more appealing to the curious adventurer. An excellent example of this can be found in an article published in the *Liberty Weekly Tribune* on December 3, 1880:

> *Few of the people who daily pass over that part of Santiago Street between the plaza and the post office, and along the eastern side of the cathedral, are aware that it is paved with human bones. Such, however, is the case.*
>
> *Many years ago, this was a public burying ground; that was before Albuquerque ever dreamed of being a railroad town or even growing to the magnitude of a major city. But as years passed by and the population increased, the streets were gradually extended out into the cemetery until a few years ago, when it was opened out and became the most frequented thoroughfare of the town.*
>
> *When the bodies were placed there, they were probably buried about two feet underground, but the sand has been loosened by traveling over it and carried away by the winds until they have come to the surface.*
>
> *The severe windstorm of Thursday swept the street perfectly clean down to the solid earth, and yesterday several complete human skeletons could*

be distinctly traced in the middle of the street while scores of white circles showed where reposed skulls of the former inhabitants of Albuquerque, the top worn away by constant contact with hoofs and wheels. In one case, the teeth which were still perfectly intact protruded above the surface, and the writer stooped down and pulled out two or three of them. Anyone desirous of seeing this ghastly pavement can do so by visiting the spot at any time after a windstorm, and all who do will understand Shakespeare when he says: "Imperial Caesar, dead and turned to clay, might stop a hole to keep the wind away."

This particular location in Old Town is now one of the many stops on the local ghost tour. However, New Town also has its share of defiled burial grounds. According to local folklore, one of the most haunted and infamous places in Albuquerque is contained within Fairview Cemetery. The oldest section of this graveyard is on its northern boundary, where more than twelve thousand people are laid to rest. Buried in this part of the cemetery are veterans of the Spanish-American War and many of New Mexico's former politicians. Seventeen of Roosevelt's Rough Riders are also interred here, as well as Fransisco Perea, a friend of Abraham Lincoln. At Ford's Theatre, he was present the night that the president was shot, occupying the box directly below his.

Another infamous resident of the cemetery is Kiku Honda, a prostitute who worked for Lizzie McGrath in one of her more scandalous brothels in New Town. Kiku was murdered on July 12, 1896. Her sad story was detailed in the *Albuquerque Journal* only a few days after her death:

Kiku Honda, the murdered Japanese woman, was to have been buried yesterday morning, but a dispatch from her brother at Portland saying he would be here caused the program to be changed at the last moment. This, however, did not prevent Rev. A. Adkinson from holding service over the remains.

The coroner's inquest was resumed yesterday afternoon in the council chambers at the city hall. The following witnesses were examined: Mabel Yamista, William Anderson, Policeman Glover, Marshal Fornoff, Captain Tyler, and Aggie Adams.

It appears from the evidence that Trout, who is under suspicion of having committed the murder, accompanied the Honda woman to Mabel Yaunsta's, three doors away, at 11:30 o'clock, where the three of them had lunch. After they both left there, the Honda woman returned to her rooms, but it is not

One of the two areas dedicated to veterans, some of which participated in the Spanish-American War. *Photo by author.*

known whether Trout accompanied her or not; the supposition is that he did. From this time until 1:30 o'clock, Trout's time has not been accounted for. It was then he accosted Policeman Glover and said, "Something is wrong at Mabel's; rapped twice, but no one responded."

Glover, accompanied by Trout and William Anderson, a colored man, went at once to No. 205 North Third Street, and while Glover remained at the front door, he sent Anderson and Trout around to the back door. They found it open, with a lamp dimly burning in the middle room. Trout entered first, picked up the lamp, and went into the front room, set the lamp on a commode when he turned up the light. On entering the front room, he could not possibly have reached the commode without having stumbled over the corpse, but it appears that he did not do so, although it was dark at this time. When he reached the commode and turned up the light, he turned his head to the left and exclaimed: "She's dead, Oh, she's dead!" He seemed to be quite familiar with the location of the body, although he was not supposed to know that a murder had been committed up to this time.

Policeman Glover at once sent for Dr. Hope and Marshal Fornoff. They began an investigation and found the bed had been occupied, and a silk handkerchief, which has several times been identified as belonging to Trout, was found on the bed. A handkerchief covered with blood with a hole in the center was found between the springs and the mattress of the bed. This handkerchief had contained the piece of lead with which the death blows were dealt, and the lead had worked its way through the handkerchief. This was later found in the outhouse, having been slipped into the woman's stocking. Other damaging evidence was the fact that tracks in the mud leading to the outhouse exactly corresponded in size and shape to the shoes Trout wore. He also claimed he could not be admitted to the house, whereas a latch key was found in his pocket. It appears from the evidence of Captain Tyler that two weeks previous to the death of the Honda woman, she and Trout had quarreled, at which time he said: "If you ever make a break like that again I will beat your brains out." From the evidence, it would look as though he had carried out his threat. The undergarments of Trout were produced, and each one contained a drop of blood upon it. Other important evidence will be introduced today, and some startling development may be looked for.

Despite its remarkable history, the cemetery has also been heavily vandalized over the years. Tombstones have been knocked over or spray-painted. Some have been busted apart and even moved. So, it should come as no surprise that many people believe that it is haunted.

Many sightings of ghostly phenomena have been reported over the years, some of which have occurred in broad daylight. The direct access to the older section of the cemetery is a rather run-down road, surrounded on one side by a wooded area. In short, it is an extremely creepy looking place.

One of the first stories told to me about the cemetery was by a young woman who worked at a local metaphysical bookstore. She was very animated when she told her story, and she is very content that she has seen a ghost. She said:

When we first entered the old section of the cemetery, we noticed a lady walking toward us. When I looked at her, her face was very pale, and she looked to be in her mid-twenties. She was very quiet and never spoke a word to us. She was wearing a long, heavy dress, which looked quite outdated. In her hand was a medium basket, which held some dead flowers. She stood there for a minute or two, just looking straight ahead. It seemed she was in another world. The strange part was that it was about ninety degrees, so no one would be dressed up in this type of clothing because it would be too hot for them. Just her being there and not speaking a word, it gave me this chill down my back, and also, I'm sure my family felt the same way. She finally left, and she went out of the archway of the cemetery. I went to see where she had gone, but when I did, she had vanished. There was no way that she could have walked down the sidewalk that fast. After the lady left, we all felt like we had just experienced something very weird. When I think about it, I really can't say why I think this happened. I don't see things like this every day. But let me tell you, this is something I would not want to see again.

Another story concerning an unusual encounter at the graveyard occurred late one summer evening. For obvious reasons, as you will discover, the persons involved in this episode wish to remain anonymous, so I'll refer to them as Bill and Jim:

We were walking through the cemetery when we spotted two policemen in their cars. We both dropped to the ground in fear that we would receive a trespassing ticket since it's illegal to be in cemeteries at night. We stayed there for about two hours, hoping that the police would leave so that we could take a few pictures for souvenirs. While we were there, I saw a white glowing round object floating throughout the cemetery. I just stared, trying to catch my voice to tell my friend, but I was so shocked I couldn't speak. Finally, I was able to grab his shoulder, but by this time, it was gone. Just when I started to calm down, Jim whispers to me that he had just seen a black hooded figure about six feet tall walking through the cemetery. We held on to each other, convincing one another it was only our imaginations. I was getting terrible vibes off this cemetery; whatever was there, I felt that it was evil and capable of anything. I was about to say, "Forget the pictures. Let's just go," but finally, the cops left. So, after lying in there for two hours, we were finally able to get out of there. That's when I saw a white mist out of the corner of my eye just floating about. The unusual thing was that it disappeared when I looked at it directly. I convinced myself it was only my imagination, took a few pictures, and swiftly went on my way.

Another strange event was witnessed one evening by a woman named Maria and her nephew Steven:

This is a true story, and we are still freaked out by what happened. My nephews were spending the weekend with my husband and myself at our home in Albuquerque. At the time, they were fourteen and eleven, and both children liked to tell and hear scary stories. One night, my nephew Steven and I needed to go to the grocery store to pick up a few snacks to go with a video we had rented earlier that day. On the way out the door, I told

A twisted wrought-iron fence that protects one of the graves in the cemetery. *Photo by author.*

Steven that we should drive Ronnie, his little brother, to the old graveyard in Fairview Cemetery, and we can all tell scary stories along the way. My husband overheard us and said, "Don't go back there today; it is too dark and dangerous for you three alone."

We said, "Ok, we won't," and promised not to go.

Little Ronnie decided to stay home, so Steven and I were on our way to pick up some goodies for the fellows. Forgetting the promise we made, we headed for the graveyard anyway. When I approached the cemetery, it looked unusually dark, perhaps due to the stormy weather earlier in the day. As we drove toward the graveyard, we noticed two people, a young man and a lady, walking toward us in the middle of the street. They were both dressed in white and just seemed to stand out. I slowed the car down, and I thought how strange it was for them to be dressed in the same manner and all-white clothing. They walked to the side of the road, and as I passed them, we noticed the road ahead looked darker and darker, so we decided to turn the car around.

In a matter of only a few seconds, and as I turned the car around, Steven said, "Auntie, where are those two people that were on the road?"

I pulled over to the side of the road and took a quick look. There was an open field, no cars nearby, no dark shrubs or trees. No place for them to hide or not be seen by us if they were really there. That was when we both became extremely frightened and decided to go straight to the grocery store.

When we got to the store, which is usually open twenty-four hours a day, the doors were locked. Although the lights were on, no one would let us in. By this time, we were really scared, and food or no food, we decided to go home.

The most bizarre encounter that I have ever had at the cemetery is also one of the funniest. As the sun was setting one evening, my comrade Bob Carter and I left the cemetery when, suddenly, Bob stopped to check out an unusual reading on one of the instruments. I was busy filming with a video camera when I suddenly heard Bob shout out. I turned to find Bob spinning around in midair, grabbing his behind.

"Somebody just pinched my ass!" he yelled as he landed.

We both looked down and saw the headstone of a naval officer.

"You cheeky bastard!" Bob replied as we continued our departure from the cemetery. I tried to rationalize Bob's pinch as merely being an insect bite; however, it was February, and no insects were present.

We continued walking for about twenty seconds when we both heard an unusual noise coming from behind us. To me, it sounded like a cough, but to Bob, it sounded more like a laugh. We both turned around. No one was there. We were the only ones in the cemetery.

The graveyard also has many urban legends associated with it. One of them tells of witches meeting at the crossroads in one section of the graveyard near a large crypt. Of course, it is false, but you can still hear stories about it around Albuquerque.

The "talking" tomb. *Photo by author.*

Another urban legend is the talking tomb. Supposedly, if you go up to the tallest crypt and knock on the door, someone inside will knock back at you. The effect is nothing more than an echo, but it has undoubtedly scared the daylights out of several teenagers in the past.

There is also some interesting folklore about the cemetery. The story always follows a similar structure, although the names of the people involved will most likely always be different. The story is called the Lady in Black and appears to be a variant of another popular urban legend, La Llorona.

The story I have selected involves a young man named John. He was engaged to marry a lovely young woman named Maria. Three weeks before the wedding, John had his bachelor party, and after a boisterous night of celebration, he had gotten really drunk. Although automobiles were relatively new to the city, the local police were exceptionally watchful in ensuring that the traffic laws were not broken. Not wanting to risk being caught driving under the influence, he chose to walk home from the party. He could always retrieve the family car in the morning. Besides, the crisp night air might do him some good.

Along the way, he had to pass the cemetery on Yale Street, and noticing that it would be quicker to cut across the cemetery rather than going around it, he hopped over the short wall. The shortcut also provided a means to bypass the angry dog that inhabited the far street corner.

As he was stumbling across the graveyard, he suddenly felt the need to urinate, so he did. However, he was so drunk that he failed to notice that he was urinating on a grave. The youth was too intoxicated to care when he realized what he was doing. Instead, he merely chuckled. After he was finished, he kicked the tombstone and said, "Hey, why don't you come to my wedding?" Laughing, he went on his way.

Three weeks later, John married Maria in a beautiful ceremony. However, as he entered the church, he noticed a figure, completely dressed in black, sitting in the last pew. Her face was hidden underneath a black veil, so he had no idea who it was. How strange was it for someone to wear black to a wedding? Although it seemed very odd to him, he didn't give it much thought as the celebration continued.

Later, at the reception, he noticed the same woman, seated all by herself at the last table. Becoming a little more curious, John asked his sister Mara to offer the woman some refreshments. Mara did, but the woman didn't want anything, dismissing her with a wave of her hand.

When the sun began to set, the Lady in Black got up and approached John. She told him that since he had invited her, he had to take her home.

"I'm sorry," he replied. "I do not know who you are, much less recall inviting you."

"Yes," the veiled woman said in an angry tone. "You invited me to your wedding three weeks ago, and I decided to attend."

A surge of panic filled John's brain as his memory recalled the events from that night in the cemetery. Frantically, he tried to think of what to say, what to do. There was only one option.

"Please excuse me while I tend to the other guests," he told the veiled woman. "I shall return soon to take you home."

Turning away, John rushed to the priest who had conducted the wedding and told him about the mysterious woman and what had occurred that night in the graveyard. The priest advised him to take a baby with him and to give the woman a ride home. However, it was essential to keep the baby with him at all times, no matter what the woman said.

After thanking the priest, John offered to watch Mara's baby daughter for a while so that his sister could enjoy the rest of the party. His sibling happily agreed. Picking up the child, he then headed back toward the Lady in Black.

"It is time for me to take you home," he said.

The lady glanced at the baby that he was carrying and shook her head. "You cannot bring this child with you," she declared.

John shrugged. "The baby is very attached to me and won't stay with anyone else."

The woman shook her head in disgust but said, "That is fine."

Leaving the church, John guided the lady to his car and began to drive. The veiled woman gave him explicit directions to her domicile. There was no moon that evening, which made the journey seem even more ominous.

After a short drive, she ordered him to stop in front of the cemetery. She got out of the car and motioned John to follow her.

"Please escort me to my door," she requested, standing by the automobile, waiting for him. "It is a gentleman's duty."

Reluctantly, he picked up the baby and exited the vehicle, following the woman into the dark recesses of the cemetery. After they had traveled some distance, she turned back to him and asked, "You don't remember me, do you?"

John shook his head. He did not know the name of the veiled woman.

"Do you remember this grave?" she asked, pointing to a small tombstone near her feet.

John's heart skipped a beat when he saw it. It was the grave that he had urinated on that night after his bachelor party.

"A while ago, you came to this place and disturbed my peace," the woman said. "I was going to take you back into my grave so that you could suffer the punishment, but I cannot, for you have an innocent with you. You must learn to respect the dead."

The Lady in Black then stepped on the grave and removed her veil. Her face was a bare skull, and her hands were nothing more than bone and rotten flesh.

Screaming, John clutched the child and ran as fast as he could out of the graveyard. When he got back to the car, he drove quickly away until arriving back at the church, the only place where he would be safe. It seems that some people must always learn things the hard way.

I find it intriguing that such folktales are found in neglected cemeteries. It is a folk belief that identifies and teaches practical functions. It stresses respect for the dead in a cultural context and the need to maintain a degree of sacredness to their last resting places.

10

Haunted Hill

One of the fascinating "haunted" places in Albuquerque is known simply as Haunted Hill. Located at the end of Menaul Street in the foothills, it is known for various urban legends. There are many stories associated with the hill, told by visitors who were brave enough to venture up there after dark. Many of them say that the hill is haunted by the apparition of an older man who used to live in a cave at the top of the hill. He would come down from the hill into town on the weekends and entice prostitutes back to his dirty abode. Once he had the woman inside his cave, he would murder her and bury her body near an arroyo located close by.

The apparition carries a lantern, and supposedly, it can be seen at night, swinging back and forth as it moves down the trail. People also claim that you can hear screaming, footsteps and the sound of bodies being dragged down to the arroyo.

Another specter that haunts the hill is called the Calling Woman. While details of the story vary from storyteller to storyteller, this is the basis of the legend.

Long ago, there was a hardworking man who had a terribly nagging wife. She always spent more money than what was brought into the household, and she complained about practically everything that he did. He was lazy. He didn't make enough money. He couldn't cook. He couldn't fix anything right. Day and night, her nagging ensued, making the man's life a living hell. He seldom argued in his own defense, for he had learned that it was only a waste of time and often made things worse.

Haunted Hill. *Photo by author.*

However, the poor man had one blessing. He often trapped game up in the mountains, and he owned a small cabin up in the foothills where he could have peace and solitude. After a while, it no longer mattered if he even caught anything, as he enjoyed the blissful hours alone while he checked his traps.

One weekend, he was preparing to leave for the cabin when his wife decided that she would accompany him.

"I know that you're wasting time up there. I'd bet that you do nothing but sleep anyway," said the wife. "How do I know what you do up there? This time I'm going to keep an eye on you."

The man was quite distraught. He knew that his week of peace was doomed. His only hope was that his wife would find the rustic conditions of the cabin so awful that she would leave the next morning. He was in for quite a disappointment.

When the man and his wife finally arrived at the cabin, she did indeed complain about the conditions. However, she made it quite clear that she was staying and began comprising a list of "chores" that needed to be done about the property.

"I knew it! Look at this rat hole! You and your lazy ways!" she harped at him. She scattered about the cabin with a disgusted look on her face.

"I have traps to set!" he protested. But she ignored his words.

"Well, you can't set traps after dark, so you'll do the chores then," she coldly replied.

For the next several days, the poor man labored. In the morning, he would set off to check his traps, enjoying the brief amount of privacy that it gave him. In the evening, he did the chores around the cabin, ever under the watching eye of his nagging wife.

Finally, the day came when he had to check the traps that were set farther up in the mountains, requiring an overnight camp away from the cabin. His wife was up to her typical complaining, and never in his life had he looked forward so much to sleeping on the cold hard ground.

"Stay close to the cabin," he warned her. "The arroyos around here can become mazes, and it's quite easy to get lost."

His wife took the remark as an insult.

"I can take care of myself, and I'll wander wherever I please!" she snapped back.

Once again, the man bit his tongue as he quickly gathered his things and departed, his wife's complaining voice gradually fading off as he went along.

Content with his solitude, the man took his time checking the distant traps. A two-day excursion turned into three. Finally, on the third day, he set off back toward the cabin.

"Hello!" he called out when the cabin came into view. But there was no answer from his wife.

"Hello!" he called again as he swung open the door, looking inside.

However, his wife was not there.

The grate of the fireplace was cold, no meal was prepared and it became apparent that his wife had wandered off and become lost. He chuckled. Finally, he could argue that he was right about something, and she was wrong.

Feeling free and in good spirits, he lit a fire and began to make a meal for himself. As he moved a kettle over to the fire, he suddenly felt a cold chill race through his spine. There, in the flames, was the face of his wife, looking menacingly at him. As he stared in disbelief, the spectral image spoke to him.

"Stuffing your face instead of searching for me to give me a decent burial! You lazy dog!"

"Burial?" the man gasped as he moved backward.

"Find me!" sneered his wife. "You sniveling—" Before she could finish her insult, the man grabbed a cup full of water and threw it on the flames. With a loud hiss, the fire sputtered out, and the flaming head vanished.

With a sigh of relief, the man sat at the table, alone once again. He no longer felt hungry. Could his wife really be dead? Somehow that thought made him feel odd, feel happy. She was gone forever! Then, off in the distance, he heard the loud clap of thunder. The spring monsoon had arrived, and a wall of black approached the cabin from the river valley. The hour was getting late, so he decided to lie in bed while the storm passed. Then he would decide what to do.

The frigid rain violently struck the cabin as the wind howled and shrieked, carrying the screeching voice of his wife with it.

"Find me, you lazy dog! Find my body!"

The man put his fingers in his ears and yelled back at the ghostly voice.

"Leave me be!" he screamed as he sat on the bed. Rocking back and forth, he started humming, trying to drown out the specter.

But the voice only grew louder.

"You're wasting time. Get out and find me!"

Finally, the man could stand no more. He knew that he would not be able to rest until he found the body of his wife. Grabbing a lantern and lighting it, he grudgingly walked out into the pouring rain, following the sound of the ghostly voice.

"Find me…" the wife's voice wailed in the distance. The rain made it practically impossible to see, and several times, he almost lost his footing, sliding downward toward one of the arroyos.

This is what must have happened, he thought to himself. She must have fallen down one of the arroyos and killed herself—stupid woman.

The wind picked up, and the rain pelted his body in waves of cold, making it difficult to pinpoint the exact location of his wife's shrieking voice. Just when he thought that the voice was getting closer, it would suddenly change direction. Sometimes it was off to the left; at other times, it seemed to come from behind. Then very quickly, it became quite clear.

"Find me! Find me, you worthless bastard!"

The voice was louder and seemed to come from his left. He turned and stumbled as he slid deep down into a wet arroyo. The lantern fell from his grasp, landing in a small stream of water, extinguishing it.

"I can't find you!" he yelled into the wet darkness. There was no reply.

The wind blasted down through the arroyo. Then there it was, very faint, her voice. At first, it sounded like she was laughing, a laugh that was gradually building up into a scream. He fumbled about in the mud, trying to turn around. He was sure that he had finally found her. The noise grew louder as he glanced over his shoulder. The last thing he saw was a wall of water as it ripped down the hillside. The arroyos are known to flood. They are known to be deadly.

It has been many years since then. Few wander around the haunted hill at night, but those who do often hear a woman's voice on the wind. Sometimes they may even see the ghost of an old man who is doomed for eternity to look for the voice of his lost wife, his spectral lantern swaying wildly as he crosses from one arroyo to the next.

Sometimes ghost stories prompt legend trips to the locations mentioned in the tales. These personal encounters reinforce the urban legend, keeping it active in the various storytellers' collective memory. The legends continue to exist as long as people keep telling the story. One example was posted on the internet in 2018. It reads:

> *A couple of friends and I went there once to investigate. We had barely made it a couple of yards from the parking lot when a light appeared on the hill above. It was rocking back and forth and was flickering, dim then bright. It was an orange glow you couldn't miss. All of us saw it. Around the same time, we heard growling. My friend and I got this sinking feeling, and I was suddenly afraid for my life. We continued up the path until a rock had been thrown at us. We were not able to determine which direction it had come.*
>
> *I was in tears for no reason, and the others were freaked out. So we headed back to the car and watched the hill. The light disappeared and then reappeared on the other side of the hill. This light was the same flickering*

The trailhead marker that leads to Haunted Hill. *Photo by author.*

swinging orange, only this time it was coming down the mountain very fast. That was enough for us, and we left as quickly as possible.

Later we reviewed our video and audio footage. We managed to catch a female scream, several deep male groans, and other unexplainable howls. I absolutely refuse to ever go back there. It felt as if something was watching me the entire time there and even a while after. I couldn't even begin to explain the feeling I had in the hills. All I can say is that I felt devastated and knew I was going to die. This place is not a safe place.

A lot could be said for the power of suggestion. What you expect influences your behavior and perceptions. Here is another story that was posted on the internet. Is this account something of a paranormal origin or only a nocturnal visit from the local wildlife?

This place scared the crap out of me. My half brother, some friends, and I were going to go there to smoke and talk without having to worry about people, but even driving up there, I felt uneasy and wanted to go somewhere else. When we got to the parking lot, I didn't want to get out of the car. It was dark, probably darker than it should have been. I felt like multiple things were watching us. My brother decided we should walk up the hill, and I reluctantly followed because I didn't want to be left alone there. Some of my other friends were getting creeped out, and we kept hearing rustling. Finally, I heard a growl right behind me. I've always been a very anxious person, so I flipped out. I started running to the car and one of my friends, who heard it too, was right next to me. We got in the car, and as soon as the others caught up, we got out of there. I couldn't help but feel we were being followed for miles after we left.

Although the legends surrounding this area are only folklore, there are quite a few people who believe that there is something dark and paranormal here. The area is easily accessible, well-traveled and used for hiking, walking and mountain biking. So, if you are up to the challenge, take a look for yourself.

11

THE ALBUQUERQUE LITTLE THEATRE

In the 1880s, with the railroad built in Albuquerque, the Santa Fe Railroad built a theater with lectures, shows and chalk-talks to improve the townspeople and tourists. The Grant Theater burned down in 1897. Another was built where Hotel Andaluz now stands.

By 1899, Elks lodge converted the old San Felipe Hotel on Gold into a theater. It opened in 1900 with a gala performance starring Lilian Russel and comedians Weber and Fields. It operated for fourteen years before it finally closed.

In 1903, the City Electric Line was established, and an amusement center was opened and known as Transaction Park. There were light operas directed by the talented singer and dancer Rose Berry. By 1927, the Chrystal Theater was the only remaining playhouse. It was eventually closed by a city ordinance because the plaster ceiling was falling on the customers.

The KiMo Theater was built in 1927, primarily as a picture house. Eventually, a stage was added because it wanted to attract roadshows. Later that year, Dr. George St. Clair, a professor of English at the University of New Mexico, started the Department of Theater Arts, Speech, Communications and Drama.

The Albuquerque Little Theatre was founded in 1930 by a group of civic-minded citizens led by Irene Fisher, a reporter and the society editor for the *New Mexico Tribune*. The concept of a local theater group was created when Fisher attended a lecture by Kathryn Kennedy O'Connor, a professional

The stage and auditorium sections of the theater. *Photo by author.*

actress who moved to New Mexico in 1927 for health reasons. Fisher organized and led the campaign to raise money for an operating budget of $1,000, and O'Connor was hired as the theater's director. The Albuquerque Little Theatre spent its first six years at the KiMo Theatre in downtown Albuquerque. As early as 1916, little theaters had been starting up all over the United States. New York had become too expensive for many people, and second- and third-rate road companies started offering the theater experience to the masses. The phrase "little theater" is not precisely accurate. It should be called the community theater. The name "little" became attached to any theater that was not fully commercial by the 1920s.

During Mrs. Kennedy O'Connor's lecture at the University of New Mexico, she mentioned the theater, which caught the attention of a reporter named Ms. Fisher, who wrote editorials in the local newspaper that stressed the need for a theater in Albuquerque. This raised awareness, and soon, the community began raising funds. The first production was a play called *Rain*, starring Mrs. O'Connor and directed by her husband. All of the productions were done at the KiMo in hopes of raising enough money to build their own local theater, one that would only perform plays and not show moving pictures.

Mr. Clinton Anderson, a U.S. senator, said there were only two good things in Albuquerque: the salubrious climate and the Little Theatre. He soon became the president of the Little Theatre Board of Directors.

Mr. Herbenstriet donated a lot to build the Little Theatre, located off Central Avenue and near Old Town. The original building was designed by famed southwestern architect John Gaw Meem and was the first structure in Albuquerque to be built by the Works Progress Administration as part of President Franklin Roosevelt's New Deal in 1936.

Building the Little Theatre was extremely difficult. Anyone who sits in the building today knows of the day-to-day struggle and tension of locating and paying for the mortar, tin, cement and other materials used in its construction. Indeed, everybody now takes the building for granted, and some think that it is not quite nice enough.

The theater's seats were purchased by putting on a New Year's Eve party. Costing two dollars apiece, the seats are still in use today. When finally completed, the auditorium floor was made of concrete and slopes rather sharply for some ten rows and then flattens out the remaining distance to the orchestra pit, instead of having a gradual incline from the lobby doors down to the stage. The concrete presented a problem when it came to fastening down the seats. With the help of some National Youth Administration boys, James O'Connor drilled two thousand holes in the concrete in which they secured the theater seats he had purchased from the Sunshine (motion picture) Theater. Some of the actors also helped with this arduous task.

In the beginning, there were no dressing rooms. For some time, the actors and crew used an old workmen's shanty left after the building was completed and an old boxcar that James O'Connor brought from the railroad for restroom and dressing room facilities. The boxcar had been purchased for $50 and eventually burned down. However, the insurance money and funds from Mrs. Simms in the amount of $4,000 paid off all debts, and a dressing room and workshop were built. The city relinquished its authority under the basis that the building would be used for "educational purposes." The government also granted the theater freedom from taxation.

In 1930, on the opening of the Little Theatre's first play, *This Thing Called Love*, the society editors of both the *Journal* and the *Tribune* wrote magnanimously of their impressions of the audience and the show.

O'Connor retired as the theater's director in 1961, and the board named Bernard Thomas to succeed her as the Albuquerque Little Theatre's full-time director. Thomas served as the theater's director from 1961 to 1980 and starred in many of its productions, including *Teahouse of the August Moon* and *His and Hers*. He was married to Reba Thomas, who hosted a daily matinée movie on a local Albuquerque television channel. Bernard also appeared in the motion picture *Roughneck*. During Thomas's years as director, he brought many popular comedies and a fine assortment of dramas. He exposed Albuquerque audiences to some unusual fare, including the world premiere of David Madden's *Cassandra Singing*. Thomas retired in 1980 after the fiftieth anniversary season. He was replaced by his technical director, Michael Myers, who served as producing director until 1986, when Sandy Brady replaced him, and Carol Fleming was named general manager in 1988. She stayed with Little Theatre until 1996.

In March 1997, Larry D. Parker was named the Albuquerque Little Theatre's new executive director and continued producing quality theater through the 2005–6 season. The current executive director is Henry Avery. He took that role in the spring of 2008.

Later that year, the theater had an opportunity to bring extensive Broadway and community theater experience to the stage when Henry Avery was hired as executive director; shortly after that appointment, he was also named artistic director. Avery's five decades of experience and commitment to live theater have resulted in new energy that infuses every aspect of the Albuquerque Little Theatre. Our fascinating history also includes several celebrities. One of America's most beloved television personalities got her start at the Albuquerque Little Theatre, performing in our very first show in 1930. Vivian Vance won the first Best Supporting Actress Emmy Award for her role as Ethel Mertz on *I Love Lucy*. That coveted award is now proudly displayed in our lobby, a cherished gift to Albuquerque Little Theatre from Vance's family after her passing. Many other celebrities have performed on our stage over the years, including Don Knotts, Bill Daily, Ann B. Davis, Nancy Kulp and Maureen O'Sullivan, to name a few.

Another theater tradition is the ghost light. A ghost light is a small, single-bulbed light, usually a floor lamp of some sort, that shines on the dark stage throughout the night when the theater is closed and unoccupied. It's usually known as an end-of-night procedure. You might hear people say, "Hey, don't forget to put the ghost light on," before they leave the theater for the night. A night would not be complete without lighting it. So, many have asked through the years what the purpose of the ghost light in theaters is.

Its true purpose is primarily safety, in case someone is in the theater working late. It allows them to see where they're going. Stages have so many hidden places, bumps and holes. You do not want someone to accidentally fall off the stage or get injured on any working equipment if the set is being built. The light helps to avoid any of these obstacles.

In a more historical sense, the ghost light has several other reasons. It is said that every theater has a ghost. The ghost light provides light at night for any spirits to see and even perform or dance on the stage. It sounds spooky or creepy, but many have stories to share about it, and sightings of these spirits have allegedly happened.

In folklore, most of the spirits that haunt theaters are not malicious. If you think about it, a theater is a happy place. It's a theatrical and artistic space to have homed many shows and performers. So, anyone who has died in these places has no reason to feel any hate toward the buildings or their current performers. It is believed that these ghosts have an attachment to the building or might have some unfinished business, but generally speaking, the theater's spirits are kind.

However, sometimes they freak people out. The theater is historical, so these stories and past people go hand in hand because it's part of its history. Other names for the ghost light are equity lamps and equity lights. The

The grand entrance into the theater. *Photo by author.*

Actors Equity Association might have been the true originator of the ghost light, hence those names. Some stories might bring some truth to the ghost light superstition. Other people don't believe in it at all. However, it is still respected as a tradition, regardless of anyone's viewpoint. The tradition itself is a beautiful and magical custom, mostly because it's become an everyday thing that almost everyone follows. It shows respect to those of the past, and it's an honor to do so.

In addition to its superstitions, the Little Theatre is supposedly haunted by at least two ghosts. The first is Bernard Thomas, executive director for most of the 1960s and '70s, affectionately known as "Bernie" at the theater. The second is believed to be Manuel Jaramillo, a custodian and master carpenter. In accordance with his final wishes, Manuel's ashes were scattered under the stage after his death.

Ronda Lewis, the theater's resource development director, spoke with me about the unusual events that have happened in the building: "Everyone that I've talked to that has felt or experienced anything in the theater says that it has never been a malicious or threatening presence. It's almost a protective sense that we get from these experiences. I feel like these spirits are still looking after things, and they're still looking over us and making sure that we are keeping and holding the legacy and doing what we're supposed to be doing so well."

When asked if there were any other ghosts besides Manuel and Bernie, Ronda said it might be possible:

> *It may be possible that there is another ghost. Here in Albuquerque, where there's so much history in this area of town, it could be anything. I have heard a story, but I have not been able to verify this. This building was the first WPA project, and the construction was finished in 1936. Some stories say that someone fell from the scaffolding during construction. I have not been able to verify that story, so it is possible to guess where those other entities would come from. I don't know, but I think anything is possible in this area. A newspaper article from 1993 also mentions that Manuel saw the ghost of Bernie Thomas. This was about a week after Bernie had passed. Manuel was walking the building doing his thing when he saw Bernie appear in the hallway. There's actually been a lot of activity in this little space. It's near a dressing room, and he saw Bernie walking by. He nodded to Manuel and vanished. Another active area is the rehearsal space, which is where we rehearse a show when we have another one on stage. I was told by someone from our cast last night when they were rehearsing*

Amadeus *that just a few weeks ago, they were in the rehearsal room when the heavy door at the bottom of the stairs slammed shut very loudly. As you can see, there's nothing that would blow that door closed, so that was kind of unusual.*

Several other members of the staff have been kind enough to share their strange experiences as well. Here are their accounts:

Lando Ruiz here. I am the resident sound designer here at the theater. I am a night owl by nature, and I will often do my sound work late after everyone else has left so I can focus on the sound effects and speakers. This incident happened one night as I was preparing sounds for Little Shop of Horrors. *I had just redone the cabling for the speakers and needed to test that I did everything correctly. I played some non-lyrical music and started to get into the groove of the music and begin to relax. As I enjoyed the sounds of the subwoofer, out of the edge of my vision, I saw someone walk across the stage, and a piece of paper fall as if the sympathetic movement of someone walking past the paper moved it.*

I immediately stopped the music and had a slight moment of did I really see that? I kept looking in the direction of where I saw it. And kept listening in silence for a while. I had never experienced anything before this, so I battled myself in trying to figure out if it was an actual moment of seeing something or just the late night. Another encounter I had was when I was working on our equipment and had to check on some items in the balcony booth. I was staring out at the stage from the balcony when I heard some kind of crash in the lobby. The balcony is only separated from the lobby by a pair of doors and a straight staircase. I kept my eyes open to see if anyone tried to exit through the audience, and no one did. After a few minutes of getting the courage to go to the lobby, I noticed there was a light on that I did not remember being on prior. I continued to check the lobby area to see if someone was there and found no one. I looked around for what had fallen, as it sounded like something had broken from the fall, and once again, nothing. Normally, I would dismiss both of these instances, but knowing there have been stories in the past and sightings, seeing and hearing them made a lot of my skepticism disappear. There are not very detailed stories or much to go off of, but I genuinely believe that it would be ridiculous to rule out paranormal activity happening here at the theater.

Haunted Albuquerque

It appears that the ghosts that are rumored to haunt the building prefer to interact with people when they are alone in the theater. Here is another account that details several experiences:

My name is Amy, and I'm the production coordinator at the Albuquerque Little Theatre. I'm pretty new to the theater because I just moved here, but I am in the building quite a bit by myself to open it up. I've had two experiences of note, and I can tell you comments from others I have heard. One time I was opening the theater for Amadeus, *and as I was coming into the house from the lobby from the stage right doors, I heard a very loud voice whisper, "Hey...hey." It was coming from the sound booth we have in the corner of the house. I had not turned the house lights on yet, so it was pretty shadowy over there. I stopped and said, "Hello?" There was definitely no one else in the theater yet. Of course, no reply, so I decided to* QUICKLY *walk to the stage and into the shop area. Just as I got to the doorway from the house to the stage, I heard the same "hey" again from the sound booth. The second one wasn't as obvious, but again, I was opening up the theater for a rehearsal for* Mamma Mia, *and I knew we were going to be using the stage that night, so I went downstairs from the rehearsal room to turn on the lights and the A/C. I saw a glimpse of some movement on the stage when I turned on the work lights and then just started to feel weird. I walked back to the green room bathroom area but got an even weirder feeling, so I went up quickly to the rehearsal room, grabbed my phone, and went to wait outside until another person arrived. It wasn't a bad feeling, just a spooky one. I didn't even sit with my back to the door.*

I sat at an angle so I could make sure the door didn't open. Those were my experiences, but I have heard multiple people say they see figures on the stage. We are always careful to leave the ghost light on, but we aren't perfect with it, and I always feel uneasy when I come in and it's not on. People have also mentioned figures in the house from time to time, but I have not seen any of those personally. We definitely hear noises and figures on the edge of your peripheral vision, and it just never quite feels "empty" in the building. But no one has expressed any situations that felt strongly negative, not to me, just more like the theater ghosts of the past that watch over us. I think theater ghosts are the coolest. As long as we keep entertaining them with our productions, they get to play on our sets at night. I've been in other theaters with a more malicious feeling to them, but never at the Albuquerque Little Theatre. But just to be sure, I follow all the theater rules and greet the theater every time I get there.

Whether you chose to believe or disbelieve the tales from so many people is a choice that is left to the reader. However, they keep the memories of its history and colorful characters alive and current in the living memories of those who love the theater. I would highly recommend attending one of the theater's performances to discover it for yourself. I am confident that they will keep the ghost light on for you.

12
GHOSTLORE

Ghostlore is a term that I use to identify specific elements of folklore and superstition that involve ghosts. New Mexico has many of these, as its culture is a blend of Native American, Spanish, Anglo and Mexican. People have always had a deep fascination with death and the afterlife. As a result, ghosts and death have passed into our folklore and native culture, generating a variety of superstitions to avoid or protect oneself and family from the unknown.

For example, the custom of wearing black at a funeral has its roots in superstition. Our ancestors believed that ghosts were quite capable of returning from the grave to bother the family, so certain precautions were taken to avoid such unpleasantness. It was believed that ghosts could not see the color black; therefore, one should wear black to the funeral so that the deceased's ghost could not follow you back home. Women were particularly susceptible to this, especially the wife or mother of the deceased, so they wore black veils to conceal their identities.

Often, the route taken to the graveyard was not the most direct. It was believed that certain forms of unpleasant spirits were somehow attracted to the path of mourning, so the same route was used over and over in an effort to confine them to one locale. This same superstition was applied to known places of death, such as hanging trees. Local children were often told ghost stories about these places to keep them away from these areas.

The early New Mexicans had a particular problem with this. They feared that if they buried their dead outside in a cemetery that the local Natives would dig them back up, so they buried them inside the house itself. It makes you wonder who you may be walking over if you visit an older hacienda.

Other forms of protection against ghosts were incorporated into the house itself. All doors facing west were painted "Virgin Mary blue" to prevent spirits from entering the house. When the deceased's body was taken out of the house, it always had to be through one of the western doors.

Another protective measure was to bury bottles of beer, lined up in a row, in front of the other doors of the house. This is a spinoff of the old superstition that ghosts cannot cross bodies of running water. However, sometimes this was done to honor members of the family who had passed on.

Another custom was to hang small bells on the inside of the main door so that they ring when the door is opened and shut. For some reason, ghosts hate the sound of ringing bells and flee from the noise. This is a very ancient practice that was widespread and even crossed cultural barriers. In China, the same thing was done, except that they created wind chimes, which they hung outside of their homes and temples and for protection from spirits. There is even some evidence that suggests the ringing of church bells before a service was done to frighten away all of the evil spirits in the area so the worshipers could make it to the church unharmed.

When a death occurred in the family, there were immediate steps that had to be taken to ensure that no further deaths or bad luck would come. All reflective surfaces were covered, especially mirrors, and all clocks in the house stopped. Mirrors have always had superstitious elements associated with them. In this case, it was feared that a mirror could trap the spirit, preventing it from crossing over to the other side. The association with clocks and the life expectancy of human beings can be dated to the Medieval period and was probably brought over to New Mexico by the Spanish.

All of the windows of the house had to be opened as well. This was done to allow the spirit to leave the house. Failure to do so would only trap the spirit within, making it angry and leaving it free to haunt the family.

Other remedies for supernatural ills were developed and offered protection from ghosts, some of which were quite humorous:

- Carry a lump of bread in your pocket when walking in the dark. It will serve as an offering to ghosts, and they will let you pass.
- If you see a ghost, walk around it nine times, and it will disappear. If you can't walk around the spook nine times, crow like a rooster. The theory behind the superstition is that ghosts don't wear watches, and they'll flee if they think daylight is coming.

- Gunshots fired in each of the cardinal directions (west, north, east and south) from each corner of your house will frighten off any ghosts or evil spirits lurking nearby.
- When passing a graveyard or a house where someone has died, turn your pockets inside out to make sure you don't bring home a ghost in your pocket.
- Another way to get past a graveyard involves picking up a stone and carrying it in your right hand until you have passed the boundaries of the graveyard. Then you set the stone down, without looking back, and you may go on your way unharmed.
- Never slam a door. You might hurt a ghost who'll haunt you for the rest of your life.

Death itself was another thing that the early New Mexicans were very superstitious about. Over the years, I have heard many superstitions concerning death, which I have listed below.

- A bird in the house is a sign of a death.
- If a robin flies into a room through a window, death will shortly follow.
- Light candles on the night after November 1. The tradition states that one should be lit for each deceased relative and placed in the room's window where the death occurred.
- You must hold your breath while going past a cemetery, or you will breathe in the spirit of someone who has recently died.
- If a broken clock that has not been working chimes suddenly, there will be a death in the family.
- If a woman is buried in black, she will return to haunt the family.
- If a dead person's eyes are left open, he'll find someone to take with him.
- Dogs howling in the dark of night howl for death before daylight.
- If you dream of death, it's a sign of a birth; if you dream of birth, it's a sign of death.
- If you touch a loved one who has died, you won't have dreams about them.
- A person who dies on Good Friday will go right to heaven.

- A person who dies at midnight on Christmas Eve will go straight to heaven because the gates of heaven are open at that time.
- All windows should be opened at the moment of death so that the soul can leave.
- The soul of a dying person can't escape the body and go to heaven if any locks are locked in the house.
- If the left eye twitches, there will soon be a death in the family.
- Funerals on Friday portend another death in the family during the year.
- It's bad luck to count the cars in a funeral cortege.
- It's bad luck to meet a funeral procession head-on.
- Pointing at a funeral procession will cause you to die within the month.
- Thunder following a funeral means that the dead person's soul has reached heaven.
- Nothing new should be worn to a funeral, especially new shoes.
- Pregnant women should not attend funerals.
- If the person buried lived a good life, flowers will grow on the grave.
- If the person was evil, weeds will grow.
- If a mirror in the house falls and breaks, someone in the house will die soon.
- A white moth inside the house or trying to enter the house means death.
- If three people are photographed together, the one in the middle will die first.
- If thirteen people sit down at a table to eat, one of them will die before the year is over.
- Dropping an umbrella on the floor means that there will be a murder in the house

The local folklore also has its ghosts, urban legends told for hundreds of years and widely known. The most popular one is the tale of La Llorona, the weeper. This is a sad tale, but it lives strong in people's memories, and there are many who swear that it is true. There are dozens of variants of this story, but this one is my favorite.

Many years ago, in a humble little village, there lived a fine-looking girl named Maria. The legend says that she was the most beautiful girl in her village, but she was jaded because of that beauty, believing that she was better than everyone else.

As Maria grew older, her beauty only increased, and her pride in her allure grew just as much. She would not even look at the local young men. They simply were not good enough to be with her.

"When I marry," she would say, "I will marry the most handsome man in all of New Mexico."

Finally, one day, a man rode into Maria's village and seemed to be just the one she had been dreaming of. He was a young ranchero, the debonair son of a wealthy rancher. He was a handsome man who could play the guitar and sing beautifully.

Maria quickly decided that this was the man for her and knew the tricks to win his attention. If the ranchero spoke when they met on the pathway, she would turn her head away. When he came to her house in the evening to play his guitar and serenade her, she wouldn't even come to the window. She refused all his costly gifts and played hard to get.

Eventually, the young man fell for her tricks. "That snooty girl, Maria, Maria!" he said to himself. "I will win her heart and marry that girl."

So, everything turned out as Maria had planned. Before long, she and the ranchero became engaged, and soon they were married. At first, things were fine. They had two children, and they seemed to be a happy family together. But after a few years, the ranchero went back to the wildlife of the prairies, a life that he loved. He would leave town and be gone for months at a time, but it was only to visit his children when he returned home. He seemed to care nothing for his beautiful wife, Maria. He even spoke of abandoning her to marry a woman of his wealthy class.

As proud as Maria was, she became furious at her husband. Rejected, she also began to feel anger toward her children because he paid too much attention to them and just ignored her.

One evening, as Maria was strolling with her two children on the shady pathway near the river, her husband came by in a carriage. An elegant lady sat on the seat beside him. He stopped and spoke to his children, but he didn't even look at Maria. Then, without acknowledging her, he abruptly left, whipping the horses on up the street.

When Maria saw that, a terrible rage filled her. Seizing her two children, she picked them up and threw them into the river. As the current carried them away, she suddenly realized what she had done. Panicking, she ran down the bank of the river, reaching out her arms in an attempt to rescue them, but they were long gone, carried away by the relentless current.

The next morning, a traveler discovered the body of a beautiful woman on the river's bank, and he rushed into the village to tell the townsfolk. When they went to investigate, they found Maria's dead body. They laid her to rest on the exact spot where they had found her.

However, the first night Maria was in the grave, the villagers heard the sound of crying down by the river. They simply thought it was the wind, but the sound became louder and more localized. When the source of the noise was investigated, they discovered that it was Maria's restless spirit crying, "Where are my children?" The tormented ghost was walking up and down the riverbank, dressed in a long white robe, the exact way that they had dressed Maria for her burial. On many dark nights afterward, they saw her walk the riverbank, crying for her children.

Eventually, her name was forgotten. Instead, they called her La Llorona, the weeping woman, and by this name, she is known to this day. Children are warned to stay away from waterways after dark, as La Llorona might mistake them for one of her children, snatching them and never returning them home.

La Llorona has many appearances and shapes. Most typically, she has a seductive figure and dresses in either all black or white. She has long black hair with fingernails that are sometimes described as talons or claws. La Llorona's mournful shrouded ghost is usually seen near waterways and secluded areas such as riverbanks, lonely dark streets and wilderness areas, especially around midnight. She has even been known to entice men when they are out and about in deserted areas.

The legends of La Llorona are mostly folklore that is typical with other phantom hitchhiker stories. There may even be a basis for the legend, which occurred in Mexico City around 1550. According to that legend, an Indian princess named Dona Luisa de Olveros fell madly in love with a nobleman, Don Nuno de Montescarlos. She bore the nobleman two children, both out of wedlock. He had promised to marry her but instead married a woman of more social prominence. Insane with rage and humiliation, Dona Luisa stabbed her children to death with a dagger

An artist's rendition of Llorona, Melvin Callejas. *Wikiart.*

that Montescarlos had given her as a gift and then wandered the streets still dressed in the bloody clothing from the murders. She was eventually found and arrested. Soon afterward, she was charged with sorcery and hanged. Her ghost is forever doomed to wander the earth, searching for her murdered children.

Another piece of folklore concerns an entity known as La Mala Hora ("the evil hour"). She routinely appears as a beautiful long-haired woman clothed in a full white dress walking along the side of the road at night. Men who are unfortunate enough to encounter her are so taken by her seductive beauty that they mindlessly follow her with no concern about where she is leading them.

The few lucky men who have met La Mala Hora and have lived to tell the tale say they lost their sense of direction while following her. If they were carrying a light, it would suddenly malfunction and stop working. Fortunately, these fellows were astute enough to notice that the lovely lady they were following was not walking on the earth. Instead, she glided slightly above it, an indication of a supernatural being. Another trait that gave her identity away was that her toes faced backward. Those ill-fated men who didn't look down at La Mala Hora's feet are not as lucky and will follow her to their doom as she leads them over the edge of a cliff. If La Mala Hora is sighted on the road dressed in black, one should be especially cautious. She is far more dangerous in her black-clad form and is a harbinger of death.

In New Mexico, La Mala Hora has several different forms. The legend was studied by Aurelio Espinosa, a professor at Stanford University, who was internationally known because of his studies in Spanish and Spanish American folklore and philology. In 1910, he described La Mala Hora, or La Malogra, as an evil spirit that haunts the crossroads, stalking those who travel alone at night. The figure is so terrifying that the mere sight of her can drive a person insane.

According to Espinosa, La Malogra can also appear as a dark cloud that he described as a floating fleece of wool that expands and contracts in size before its victim. When it appears in this form, it is a sign of disaster or death.

More modern New Mexican versions of La Mala Hora describe her as a terrifying old woman dressed in black who manifests to travelers at night when a death is about to occur. Again, there are many variants of this ghost story. The place where the story begins changes from one storyteller to the next, but the destination is almost always Santa Fe.

In one version of the tale, a woman's husband is away on a business trip. Late one evening, her friend Isabella called her, sobbing and distraught. She and her husband, Enrique, were finally getting divorced, and he had moved out of the house earlier that day. The end of her marriage and the uncertainty of the future were almost too much to bear.

So, despite the late hour and the rain, the woman decided to travel to Santa Fe to comfort her friend. As she traveled down the dark, wet highway, she had the strange sensation that someone or something was watching her. She tried to ignore it but found herself looking in the rearview mirror to check the back seat. No one was there—just the sound of the highway and the rain striking the windshield.

Don't be ridiculous, she told herself, eagerly wishing that she was home in bed instead of driving on a dark, rainy highway. There was almost no traffic, and she hoped that she would reach Sante Fe soon.

As the car approached the city, she exited the highway, taking a side road that led to Isabella's house. As she approached a small crossroads, a woman stepped into the street directly in front of her car, forcing her to slam on the brakes. The car screeched to a halt just in time to avoid hitting the stranger in the road.

Startled, the driver frantically looked around for the woman. She had disappeared, and for a moment, she thought that the stranger had fallen in front of the car. As she reached for the door to check on the mysterious woman, she looked up and saw her right beside the driver's window. Her heart skipped a beat when she comprehended what she saw.

The mysterious woman was staring at her with red eyes that glowed like the fires of hell itself. Her wrinkled face was twisted and evil like some sort of demon. The driver screamed as the apparition leaped at the window, her clawed hands violently scraping against the glass. Instinctively, she slammed her foot down, pressing the accelerator to the floor. The car lurched forward, but the demon-faced woman ran alongside, striking at the window repeatedly with its talons before the car finally got away.

Glancing in the rearview mirror, she saw the demon-faced woman stop in the center of the road. A strange red light swirled around the apparition like mist, and she pointed at the car, her mouth moving as if she was saying something. The female driver jerked her attention back to the road and breathed a sigh of relief.

In record time, the terrified driver arrived at her friend's house. Still distraught over the supernatural encounter, she flung herself out of the car and frantically knocked on the door until her friend finally answered it.

"Shut the door!" the terrified driver cried frantically, rushing past her into the safety of the house.

"What is wrong?" the friend asked, slamming and locking the door shut.

After several minutes, the driver finally managed to gasp out her story. "Are you sure you were at a crossroads when you saw her?" Isabella asked cautiously.

The driver nodded, puzzled by her friend's question.

"It must have been La Mala Hora," Isabella gasped. The worry suddenly showed on her face.

"The bad hour?" the driver asked.

"This is bad!" Isabella replied. "La Mala Hora only appears at a crossroads when someone is going to die."

Ordinarily, she would have laughed at such a superstition, but the appearance of the demon-woman had really shaken her. The pair stayed awake most of the night before retiring to get a few hours of sleep.

The driver felt much better the next morning, but she could not shake the feeling of dread that grew in her all day. Neither of them mentioned La Mala Hora, but they were both thinking of her when she told Isabella that she wanted to go home. Isabella insisted on accompanying her, as she refused to drive after dark, afraid that she would see the demon-woman again when she passed the crossroads.

They left the next morning and had not been home more than twenty minutes when a police car pulled into the driveway. She knew at once what it meant, and so did Isabella.

An evening encounter with the dead. *Wikiart*.

Although the officers spoke gently, nothing could soften the horrible news. Her husband had been mugged on the way back to his hotel after dinner last night. His body had not been found until this morning. He had been shot in the head and was killed instantly.

The fact that ghost stories are still frequently told indicates that understanding all the events of one's life can be difficult, elusive, indefinite and sometimes impossible. As a narrative type, the ghost story reminds us of how dreadful and indeterminate life can be. However, metaphorically, ghost stories also say, "Who knows?"

Bibliography

"About the Theatre." City of Albuquerque. https://www.cabq.gov/culturalservices/kimo/about-the-theatre.

"Albuquerque High School." Sensagent. http://dictionary.sensagent.com/albuquerque%20high%20school/en-en.

Albuquerque Journal. "City Buy of KiMo Possible." September 30, 1976.

———. "50 Years at KiMo." Honors Landmark. April 21, 1977.

———. "Mayor Says KiMo Top City Priority." October 29, 1976.

"Albuquerque Little Theatre, Albuquerque." Inspirock. https://www.inspirock.com/united-states/albuquerque/albuquerque-little-theatre-a221275555.

"Albuquerque Little Theatre." Wikipedia. https://en.wikipedia.org/wiki/Albuquerque_Little_Theatre.

"Albuquerque Tricentennial." Fourth Grade Teachers Resource Guide. September 2005.

Bryan, Howard. "The Second Albuquerque." *New Mexico Magazine*, April 1980.

Cisneros, Sandra. "La Llorona—A Hispanic Legend." *Woman Hollering Creek* (blog). https://groupfifth.weebly.com/la-llorona.html.

"Death Superstitions." Unsolved Mysteries. http://www.unsolvedmysteries.com/usm411767.html.

"Death Superstitions Old Wives Tales Beliefs & Misconceptions." Coursinet. http://corsinet.com/trivia/scary2.html.

Bibliography

"Factoid D Answer." Albuquerque Historical Society. https://albuqhistsoc.org/factoids/dAnswfactoid.htm.

"Frank Bond." Wikipedia. https://en.wikipedia.org/wiki/Frank_Bond.

Garcez, Antonio. *Adobe Angels: Ghosts of Albuquerque*. Santa Fe, NM: Red Rabbit Press, 1994.

"Ghosts of Albuquerque, New Mexico." Legends of America. https://www.legendsofamerica.com/nm-albuquerqueghosts.

Goldstein, D.E., S.A. Grider and J.B. Thomas. *Haunting Experiences: Ghosts in Contemporary Folklore*. Logan: Utah State University Press, 2007.

Gorney, Carole. "KiMo: A Past, Future Treasure." *Albuquerque Journal*, September 29, 1977.

Hauck, Dennis William. *The National Directory of Haunted Places*. New York: Penguin, 1996.

"Haunted Hill—Menaul Boulevard." Haunted Places. https://www.hauntedplaces.org/item/haunted-hill-menaul-boulevard.

"History." Albuquerque Little Theatre. https://albuquerquelittletheatre.org/about-us/history.

"The History of the Ghost Light." *OnStage Blog*. https://www.onstageblog.com/editorials/2020/3/25/the-history-of-the-ghost-light.

"Hotel Andaluz." Wikipedia. https://en.wikipedia.org/wiki/Hotel_Andaluz.

"Hotel Andaluz Albuquerque, Crio Collection by Hilton." Trip Advisor. https://www.tripadvisor.com/ShowUserReviews-g60933-d92752-r168246646-Hotel_Andaluz_Albuquerque_Curio_Collection_by_Hilton-Albuquerque_New_Mexico.html.

"Hotel Andaluz Albuquerque New Mexico Hotel Features." Gayot. https://www.gayot.com/travel/hotels/laposada.html.

"Investigation of the KiMo Theater, Albuquerque, NM." Southwest Ghost Hunters Association. http://www.sgha.net/nm/KiMo_Theater.pdf.

KiMo Theater History and Ghost Story Pamphlet. KiMo Theater.

"La Mala Hora." Ultimate Camp Resource. https://www.ultimatecampresource.com/campfire-stories/scary-campfire-stories/la-mala-hora.

Las Cruces Sun News. "Albuquerque Theater Blast Kills Boy, Injures Seven." August 3, 1951.

"Mexican Monstresses: La Mala Hora" *Multo (Ghost)* (blog). https://multoghost.wordpress.com/2015/08/17/mexican-monstresses-la-mala-hora.

Bibliography

Mount Calvary Cemetery, Albuquerque, New Mexico. http://bernalillo.nmgenweb.us/cemeteries/mtcalvary/mtcalvaryaaal.htm.

"Mt. Calvary Cemetery and Mausoleum." Genealogy Village. https://nmahgp.genealogyvillage.com/bernalillo/bemtcal1.htm.

Myrick, David. *New Mexico's Railroads*. Albuquerque: University of New Mexico Press, 1990.

New Mexico–Arizona Wool Warehouse. National Register of Historic Places Inventory—Nomination Form. FHR-8-300 (11-78). https://npgallery.nps.gov/pdfhost/docs/NRHP/Text/81000400.pdf.

"Railroad Boom." Albuquerque Historical Society. https://albuqhistsoc.org/SecondSite/pkfiles/pk220railroadboom.htm.

Rule, Leslie. *Coast to Coast Ghosts*. N.p: Andrew McMeel Publishing, 2001.

"Sandee Saunders: Headless in Hatch (1972)." Club Records. https://www.clubbo.com/1972-sandee-saunders.

Simmons, Marc. *Albuquerque, A Narrative History*. Albuquerque: University of New Mexico Press, 1982.

"Statehood Transportation." Albuquerque Historical Society. https://albuqhistsoc.org/SecondSite/pkfiles/pk125stathoodtranspor.htm.

"Transportation and Communication, 1945–Now Highways." Modern Transportation. https://albuqhistsoc.org/SecondSite/pkfiles/pk126moderntransport.htm.

Transportation U.S. Territorial Period, 1846–1912. Albuquerque Tricentennial: An Illuminating Experience. https://albuqhistsoc.org/SecondSite/pkfiles/pk124territravlcomm.htm.

"Wool Warehouse (Albuquerque, New Mexico)." Wikipedia. https://en.wikipedia.org/wiki/Wool_Warehouse_(Albuquerque,_New_Mexico).

"Wool Warehouse Theater." HauntedHouses. http://www.hauntedhouses.com/states/nm/wool_warehouse_theater.htm.

About the Author

Cody Polston is the author of multiple books on history and paranormal topics. He is one of the Southwest Ghost Hunter's Association founders and has been investigating paranormal claims since 1985. For his entire life, he has been fascinated by the unknown and specifically by paranormal activity such as ghosts and poltergeists. However, he remained skeptical and insisted on the use of science in his investigations. Because of his skepticism, many local ghost hunters gave him the nickname "Hitman" due to his ability to rationally discover natural causes behind many hauntings. Through this research, hands-on investigative work and skepticism, Polston became one of the most infamous ghost hunters of the American Southwest.

Visit us at
www.historypress.com